Praise for the Book

I run one of the most popular blogs on Kindle publishing and I read everything on the topic. This is the best book on the subject. Read it religiously, take those nuggets and act! You will be the next financially successful authorpreneur.
– **Dave Chesson** | Kindlepreneur

Write and Grow Rich by Alinka Rutkowska, et al. is a necessary addition to any writer's shelf.
– **Readers' Favorite**

Building a business around your writing is no simple task. It requires the same discipline, resilience and self-belief as for any startup. This book, however, gives you a serious leg-up. It's loaded with insights from authors and entrepreneurs that have been where you are now – and are achieving what you soon hope to be. Read it. Highlight it. And then start implementing. Your writing deserves it.
– **Kimberley Grabas** | YourWriterPlatform.com

Write and Grow Rich

Secrets of Successful Authors and Publishers

Alinka Rutkowska
with
Steve Alcorn, Alexa Bigwarfe, Lise Cartwright, Bryan Cohen, Amy Collins, Claire Diaz-Ortiz, Derek Doepker, Debbie Drum, Susan Friedmann, Marc Guberti, Daniel Hall, Adam Houge, Christine Kloser, Donna Kozik, Jason Ladd, Kristen Joy Laidig, Sally Miller, Derek Murphy, Kirsten Oliphant, Caitlin Pyle, Jyotsna Ramachandran, Matt Stone, Summer Tannhauser, Ash Akshay Goel, and Susmita Dutta

Leaders Press

Copyright © 2018 Alinka Rutkowska

All rights reserved. Published in the United States by Leaders Press.

www.leaderspress.com

Secrets of Successful Authors and Publishers

All rights reserved. No part of this book may be reproduced or transmitted in any form or by any means, electronic or mechanical, including photocopying, recording, or by an information storage and retrieval system – except by a reviewer who may quote brief passages in a review to be printed in a magazine or newspaper – without permission in writing from the publisher.

ISBN 978-1-63735-356-1 (pbk)
ISBN 978-1-63735-355-4 (ebook)

Library of Congress Control Number: 2018912807

To you who know that if you can write, you can grow rich

CONTENTS

Start Here... 1

PART 1: AUTHORS 5
ADAM HOUGE: Many Streams Create a River 7
BRYAN COHEN: I Pushed Harder........................ 17
DEREK MURPHY: Hone Your Craft Until You're the Best.......... 25
MATT STONE: Treat Your Book Like Your Life's Work 35

PART 2: COMMUNICATORS................................. 45
CLAIRE DIAZ-ORTIZ: I Started to See
What it Meant to Have a Voice Online.................................. 47
KIRSTEN OLIPHANT: I Release My Inner Simon Cowell 55
MARC GUBERTI: The More I Know, The More I Can Share 65
SUMMER TANNHAUSER: They Want to Hear from You 73

PART 3: MARKETERS 83
AMY COLLINS: Do it Anyway 85
DEBBIE DRUM: The Cream Rises to the Top 93
DEREK DOEPKER: Make Your Cause
Greater than Your Comfort 103
SUSAN FRIEDMANN: Out Pops Your Bonny Baby Book 113

PART 4: TEACHERS.. 123
ALINKA RUTKOWSKA: Like an Army Tank.......................125
DONNA KOZIK: Teach and the Money Will Follow 137
JYOTSNA RAMACHANDRAN: Too Lazy to Write.................147
KRISTEN JOY LAIDIG: I Feel What I Want to Do Before I Do It 155

PART 5: TRAINERS 165
ALEXA BIGWARFE: Ditch the Negative Nancies 167
DANIEL HALL: Strive for Excellence, Not Perfection 177
LISE CARTWRIGHT: Done is Better than Perfect..................183
SALLY MILLER: By Constantly Researching,
I Feel Closer to My Readers 195

PART 6: TRANSFORMERS 205
CAITLIN PYLE: I Pretty Much Ignore Everyone Else 207
CHRISTINE KLOSER: What Was Missing Was Me 217
JASON LADD: Follow the Meaning 227
STEVE ALCORN: I Try to Make Each Word Count 235
ASH AKSHAY GOEL AND SUSMITA DUTTA: Your Branded
UFO, From Author to Authority..243

Start Here

Welcome to the *Write and Grow Rich* experience.

My name's Alinka Rutkowska and I'll be your guide.

Why *Write and Grow Rich*?

20 years ago, the world-famous book *Think and Grow Rich* literally fell on my head in a bookstore. Logically, I said to myself, "I can think, so I can grow rich".

Napoleon Hill's concepts have profoundly changed the way I think. Those new thoughts I started thinking became habits, which ultimately shaped my character.

Now I consider myself a financially successful authorpreneur. I've sold more than 100,000 books and I've created several six-figure funnels, which all start with a book. But back in 2010 I was probably where you are today — just getting started, figuring things out, not quite ready to leave my day job and live my dream of *writing* and *growing rich*.

Why so many points of view for you to consider?

I'll tell you a secret. I had the dream of creating this book a year and a half before I started doing anything about it. It just seemed so difficult and time-consuming. But you can only hold off going after your dreams for so long.

I wrote the first email to one of the authors of this book, telling her about my idea and she was all over it. That was enough for me to get this amazing line-up of authors to contribute to *Write and Grow Rich*.

Most of them are independently published authors with an entrepreneurial mindset, or authorpreneurs, but I also wanted to feature entrepreneurs whose writing leveraged their business so that you can see what's possible. The bottom line is there are different ways of going about writing and they can all lead to financial success.

One man's meat is another man's poison.

This is one of my favorite quotes and you'll find it holds true as you read the pages of this book. Some authors swear that their best decisions are what other authors swear are their worst.

The devil is in the details. For example, someone might say that having a mailing list is the key to their success; another author would say it's a waste of time. Such statements are simply too generic to make up your mind just yet. You will find that the author who doesn't recommend it does things very differently from the one who swears by their list of subscribers (like me).

So please pay attention to the details.

An overnight success?

As different as the authorpreneurs featured in this book are, we have one thing in common. We all started from scratch. We were not born famous or with a subscriber list in hand. We failed and got back up again numerous times and eventually… we succeeded. And so can you. Read on.

Imagine sitting in a coffee shop picking each author's brain. That's how this book is structured. You get to ask each influencer the same 12 questions and soak in their responses.

For your convenience, I've put the contributing authors into six groups, even though many belong to several of them. In the following pages you will discover the secrets of authors, communicators, marketers, teachers, trainers and transformers.

Let's get started!

PART 1: AUTHORS

ADAM HOUGE: Many Streams Create a River

I'm very excited to introduce you to Adam. We've been partnering on various ventures for authors for a few years now. We've both spoken at each other's summits and we regularly share each other's ideas with our subscriber lists.

Adam is also the mastermind behind the promotional schedule of this book, since he's an Amazon algorithm whiz.

Adam is a No.1 internationally bestselling author of more than 100 books on the Christian faith. He has hit the top of the religious charts in both the United Kingdom and the United States during his launches and has consistently outsold his competitors (such as Billy Graham, Alex Kendrick, Max Lucado and Joel Osteen) on Amazon. Adam has also written numerous other titles in many different genres under his pen names, including romance and business. Over the past three years, he has distributed more than 2,500,000 copies of his books globally through his paid and free-launch strategies.

When did you start considering yourself financially successful as an author? How long did it take after you published your first book? How did it feel and why?

The first time I felt successful as an author was when I was kicked back under a cabana on the powder white sands of Clearwater Beach, Florida. I had already made six figures as an author, most of which was made in a three-month period, leaving me to wonder, "How long will this last?" I felt as if it might be too good to be true; out of fear, I hadn't given myself a label of success yet.

I learned the ins and outs of Amazon's algorithm, and the first thing I learned about it was that it was always changing. I kicked back further in my chair, and as my skin absorbed the heat of the sun, I asked myself the obvious question, "What if I can't adapt?" I trained my eyes on the gentle blue waves of the Caribbean while my children were squealing and splashing with mommy out in the water. A glint of determination struck me. The message I'm sharing is too important for me to allow it to fail. It was then that I resolved to make this work regardless of what happens, and if others are doing it why can't I? At that moment, I realized that Amazon makes it easy to adapt. Regardless of what changes may occur, I'll always find a way to stay on top. I drifted back in my thoughts to mull over a series of changes they made. Even when there was a major change, they wanted their merchants to succeed, so they made it easy to adapt.

Since that day, I've consistently made six figures from my books every single year without fail and have gone on to make multiple six figures from my other digital products as well.

The greatest barrier to success is fear — fear of change, fear of loss, fear of not being able to progress, fear of failure. But fear is a liar. You can't succeed at something if you don't try. Michael Jordan missed the shot more than 9,000 times, yet he's one of the best basketball players to have ever lived.

Open your mind up to possibility. Whether you're brand new as an author or full-time, you can always move forward and grow. But you can never be good at something if you don't step up to do it. You can never succeed if you don't look failure in the eye. Determination is a state of heart and a quality of the most successful people on the planet. Stay focused, remain determined, keep faith.

What have been the key factors to your success and why?

The key factor for me was knowing what my audience wants or needs and how they want to have it conveyed to them, as well as where to find and connect with them. Everything in life is about positioning. Do you want to convince someone to try a new food? Or encourage them to make the right decisions? Then position your words to meet their hearts and minds where they're at. Convey that message in a way that they'd be most likely to learn and grow from it, while loving the processes of learning from you. In the end, they'll thank you and share it with others. Hence five-star ratings and word of mouth come naturally. The same goes for whether you speak a spiritual message, give a motivational message or sell a product or book.

We are always trying to sell each other something. We sell ourselves by the way we act so people will like us and become our friends. We sell our skills and abilities to recruiters that they may hire us. We sell our opinions and try to convince others to agree with us. We sell our side of an argument to convince others that we're right. And we sell books. Selling is a method of communication that should speak to the heart and emotion. It should never be sleazy or salesy but convey a message that can earn the trust, respect and serious interest of the buyer. When you understand how to do this, it becomes infinitely easier to build a product or write a book that people love, even from a fictional point of view. The more a reader can relate to the fictional character, the more they'll love the story. By knowing what people want, or what they need in order to get emotionally invested, you'll be off to a great start. This helped me, above all else, to write exceptional copy; books that motivate and inspire change; and stories that captivate. After this, I learned where to find them and then built an audience.

What has been your worst decision as an author and how did you bounce back and still get to where you are today? Did this failure set you up for your current success?

Failure is a state of mind that freezes you in a negative mental state and keeps you from moving forward. But to answer the question: I've been at this for a while so I've had several problems that have hindered me.

My biggest 'failure' to date has been a lack of diversity in traffic options and niches, as well as not working with others sooner. This led to my current success, because I don't actually view such problems as failures; I view them as learning lessons that I grow from. I had a sudden drop in income one year that was due to my mistakes. I learned that the only way to compensate and grow was to diversify.

The biggest problem many authors and entrepreneurs have is that they have a one-legged-stool strategy for their growth — one income source; one traffic stream to grow their fan base. By all means, start with just one, but after you've mastered it, incorporate others that can bring balance if the winds change. Many streams create a river. It's the same with streams of income and traffic. Have more than one book. Have more than one series. Give away more than one free thing and in more than one place. But focus on the things and the places that produce the most results fastest. Vilfredo Pareto stated that 20 percent of your actions will result in 80 percent of the desired outcome. So focus on the 20 percent that helps you grow the fastest and master it.

What has been your best decision as an author and why?

I've had a lot of key decisions that if I hadn't made, I wouldn't be where I'm at today. So it's hard to pinpoint the best decision.

The first key decision was to get started in the first place. If you don't begin, you can't enjoy the end. Just get started. But after I began, the most important decisions I've made stemmed from my learning lessons from my mistakes, such as diversifying my back list of books for my readers to purchase. I've more than 120 books and boxsets on Amazon. I've had people write to tell me that they have bought every single one of them.

How much would I have sold if I only wrote two or three books? If you have more to sell, it's easier to reach a million sales. It only takes 10,000 sales per book to reach a million sales if you have 100 books. That's easy to achieve compared to selling a million books from one stand alone. For that matter, an author with multiple series that can work together can sell more than an author with the same amount of irrelevant stand-alone books. Diversify within your niche, write a series and write well.

What is the best investment you've made as an author and why?

The best investment I've made? Well, those are several investments. First would be investing in my financial education. I've taken courses from others that cost me thousands of dollars. But I've made six figures from the concepts that I learned.

Another great investment would be in my readers and customers. I invest my time into them to make sure they are learning, growing and loving what they read. These are people, not numbers. They need to matter to you. The more invested in them you can be, the more they'll invest into you, both from a friendship/personal standpoint as well as a buying perspective. You are their celebrity. So being able to touch you feels genuinely touching for them.

Lastly, my final investment is into my partners. I wouldn't be where I'm at today without them or my readers. If, therefore, I had to identify the greatest investment, it would be in the people around me, and taking time to care sincerely about them. I've made some fantastic friends and made some money in the process. How awesome is that?!

If you were deprived of all your marketing tools and could keep only one, which would it be and why?

My email list because the money is in the list. Your fan base writes your pay check. Your livelihood, your passion, your influence and everything you are and do as a writer all begins and ends with your readers. Who are you writing for if you don't have them?

The biggest problem people have is that they don't know how to grow their list, wield it correctly and connect with their fans properly. Once they understand how to do these things, the fan base and how you minister to their needs and wants as readers (through your writing) is all that matters.

What is an unusual habit that you have as an author that helps you succeed?

I cherish the time I get to sit and do nothing. I enjoy meditating, among other things, and prefer to spend less time working and more time enjoying life and things that matter. It's not laziness that I'm talking about. I just have a habit of seeing things with regard to my time and how efficiently it's being spent so I can have more time to do what I love. This forces me to realize that the hours in a day are in short supply. Any man can make a billion dollars. But no one can have more (or less) time in a day than you. You can never get a minute more than what you already get. Life is also short. If you want to have the most impact possible, then you need to discover what can give you the most impact with the least amount of effort. As a result, I've found ways to touch more lives, sell more books and make more money than others. I've found how to grow my email list faster than others, and how to grow and scale financially faster than many of my peers.

Each hour I work is worth thousands of dollars, and I feel that my time is worth more than this. To make more money, most people work more hours. But rather than working more hours, I try to figure out ways to make each hour more valuable, more impactful and more meaningful. As a result,

I get more time to do the things that matter to me, while touching the most lives possible.

You can only do so much in one life. So the key to doing more is not working more hours but learning how to get more done with the hours you've been given. This is what it means to work smarter and not harder and if you master this, then you'll succeed at anything you put your mind to.

What would you have done differently if you were to start your career with the knowledge you have now?

I'd have made connections and partners immediately. If the money is in the list, doesn't it make more sense to leverage other people's lists? And they'll do it for no money down or out of pocket. Yes, you'll have to share the proceeds as affiliate income but there is no upfront cost whatsoever. So, if I had to start all over, even if I had $0.00 in the bank account, I could get a domain name, create a website and make a full-time income within 30-60 days. Yeah, it would cost $10-$20 to get started but I could borrow that from a friend and pay him back with the proceeds. So, for no money down at all, I could be making six figures in less than a year following that method.

What bad advice do you often hear on the subject of book marketing?

Rely on yourself. I often hear people say to make an email list and that's all you'll ever need. No, the email list is a vehicle and not a destination. It should always be growing but how you wield it determines how well you'll do. One way to wield it correctly is to use it to build your partner base. The more partners you have, the bigger your reach is.

It's infinitely easier to get 10 friends with an email list of 20,000 each who will promote you than to build an email list of 200,000 all by yourself. And your email list should be used to make connections like this and leverage other audiences so you can make the most out of what you have. Be open, therefore, to cross-promotion and helping others. The more genuine you are and the more you help others, the more they will help you. Friends are more likely to promote friends than someone they just met. So get on their radar, then get into the friend-zone!

With that said, if I could give any piece of advice, it would be to jump into a multi-author project as quickly as possible because this is how you make those connections; especially, if you are the one creating the project. Then everyone who participates will likely work with you in the future as well.

What do you do when you feel demotivated or overwhelmed?

Overwhelmed? I sit down and write everything that needs to be done. Then I flip the page and write them in order of priority. Then I write them on my calendar with an end date in mind to make sure it gets done, while breaking it down into more manageable chunks.

What's your advice for entrepreneurs who are still struggling?

Learn the Amazon algorithm. Understanding it has been key to my success as a writer. If you want to sell more books, you have to learn how Amazon gets your books in front of more eyes, and then make the best use of the methods they give you.

The second piece would be to start making multi-author boxsets and projects immediately. The more people you get connected with in your niche the better. It doesn't matter what you write (fiction or nonfiction). The more people you know, the more people there are who will promote you and the better off you'll be.

Adam has an awesome free training program that shows you how to launch bestseller after bestseller. You can find more at www.thefanbaseformula.com

BRYAN COHEN: I Pushed Harder

I've known Bryan for years. We both sent each other warm wishes for our children's births! I interviewed Bryan for my 5-Figure Author Challenge and Bryan said a good word to Jim Kukral, who invited me to speak at Author Marketing Club.

Bryan is a *USA Today* bestselling fiction and nonfiction author. As the co-host of *The Sell More Books Show*, he's shared the latest news in the writing and marketing world for 200 consecutive weeks. As a copywriter, he's co-written more than 1,200 book descriptions. He lives in Chicago with his wife and daughter.

When did you start considering yourself financially successful as an author? How long did it take after you published your first book? How did it feel and why?

There is no one true path to becoming a successful writer and entrepreneur. There are some who find a genre or a business sector that works for them before they develop the skills necessary to take things to the next level. That wasn't me at all.

Write and Grow Rich

Even as I took my last creative writing classes in college, I knew there was a big fat problem waiting for me in the real world. I was fantastic when it came to completing essays, stories and assignments from a professor. But aside from a few coddled college plays I wrote in the prior four years, I had no idea how to sit down and do the work without somebody authoritative breathing down my neck. As I left school to move to the bright lights and chilly winters of Chicago, it didn't take long to realize that if I was going to find success, it would be through becoming a self-starter.

During my first three years in Chicago, I drifted from temp work to part-time data entry to donning the green apron of a Starbucks barista. By early morning (around 5 a.m.), I soaked up the caffeinated aroma, and by night I sat in front of my computer and hated myself. I wanted to write. It didn't matter what I wrote exactly; I just wanted to turn the blinking cursor into something creative and inspired. I wanted to become successful creatively and financially. I just didn't know how.

I bided my time performing improv comedy in dimly-lit clubs and bars, but unless I hit the top 0.001 percent of comedians who got onto *Saturday Night Live*, I would have to find an alternative. A few years after I left school, I somehow discovered freelance writing. I found a site that would pay me $15 for every 400-word how-to article I submitted. After working out the math, I figured out that I could pay my bills, start to chip away at my college debt, and stow a little bit in the bank if I wrote eight articles a day, every day no matter what.

My necessity for cash pushed me through any writer's block. I stuck in my headphones, listened to movie soundtracks on

Pandora, and set a countdown clock with E.ggtimer.com to push myself to get faster and faster. I knew the more articles I wrote, the sooner I could stop feeling like such a failure. At first, it took me 45 minutes to write a single article. As I refined my process, I was able to tackle three per hour at my best. I started to wonder if I was actually worth more than my Starbucks minimum wage.

Those were the days when I developed my out-of-school work ethic. Sometimes I got into an incredible flow state. Other days felt impossible — "I'll never amount to anything, so what's the point?" I persevered and eventually found writing work that paid me more for fewer hours. I then just needed to do something worthwhile with those hours.

In the midst of my freelance quest, I'd haphazardly published a blog about creative writing. Around the time that my paid writing fell into line, I started to see traffic on my site. After about two years of blogging, it seemed that most of the people that headed to my articles wanted one thing and one thing only — creative writing prompts to push through their own writer's block. I was lucky. Writing these prompts was just like coming up with scene ideas for improv comedy. It was almost as if my life experience had trained me to write prompts. If that's what the people want, I would be happy to provide them with it.

After writing more than 70 pages of prompts and seeing my traffic rise, I wondered if posting the prompts for free was the best use of my tireless efforts. The first article I read about self-publishing taught me to create a PDF of 1,000 prompts with a $10 price point for sale on my site and see what happened. My future mother-in-law was my first sale... and for a while, she was my only sale. When it looked like my PDF with the world's ugliest cover wasn't going to fill my income gap, I hunted for another option. I don't know how ebooks and Kindle Direct Publishing had evaded me to that point but I jumped on the process like a dog on a bone.

With a new cover created by my talented future wife, I repackaged the content and put the book up on Amazon in September 2010. No sales came in during the first 30 days. I changed tactics and linked all 150+ pages on my website to my hopeful book sales page. Orders slowly started to trickle in. I pushed harder, setting up guest blog posts on every writing website that would have me. Sales increased. By January 2011, my little book in a little niche in the corner of the massive Internet started to sell a copy a day. With my blog tour and site in full swing, that number grew to 20 sales a day by the middle of 2011.

What has been your worst decision as an author and how did you bounce back and still get to where you are today? Did this failure set you up for your current success?

Between my growing freelance writing and my steady sales, I had a choice to take things to the next level or rest on my laurels. Unfortunately, I chose the latter.

Three years later, the bottom started to fall out of my comfortable existence. The later prompts books I wrote never reached the heights of the first one, and sales began to slump. I'd now written thousands of blog posts for a variety of publications, but my earnings had only nudged up slightly with each passing quarter. If I'd used the self-starter mentality built in my first few years after school, I could've multiplied my success three times over. Instead, I got lazy and just watched the passive income depositing into my account drop lower and lower. It wasn't until my earnings dropped into the "I better consider moving back home" territory that my entrepreneurial fire came back.

I started networking with other self-published authors who catered to writers. I used the theatrical skills from my past to organize online events that got my name out to thousands of authors. One of those contacts led to the creation of *The Sell More Books Show*, which we vowed to make different from anything else that was out there. That meant more work on our parts, but I'd learned from my dark period that shying away from hard work wasn't going to do me any favors.

I stuck to a regular schedule, which included going to a writing co-op every morning to write fiction. I finished four novels within a year and upgraded my freelancing to a new position ghostwriting for publications, such as *Entrepreneur*, *Fast Company* and *Inc*. Between the podcast, the fiction and the freelancing, there weren't many hours left in the day, but income was steady and life was pretty good.

I still felt like something was missing though. It took a friend to explain exactly what that was.

What has been your best decision as an authorpreneur and why?

I initially heard about the concept of masterminds from blogger Steve Pavlina and I'd learned more through extensive personal development reading and audiobook listening. But it wasn't until late 2014 that I joined my first group. Talking about my business and my writing twice a month with like-minded authorpreneurs allowed me to get feedback on all of my harebrained ideas. And it also gave my fellow group members a chance to find opportunities I'd never even considered.

Simon Whistler, of Rocking Self Publishing, looked at all the freelancing I did and the weekly podcasting I did for authors and noticed the obvious disconnect. He asked why I was all over the board when I could just focus on one audience. I didn't have a good answer for him, of course, as I'd mostly stumbled into every single part of my business. When he suggested I ditch the freelancing and just start writing content for authors, the light bulb went on in a big way.

I didn't hesitate. I created a sales page, linked it up to a spreadsheet, and promoted the product on my podcast. I didn't charge much at the time and that's probably part of the reason I sold more than 100 descriptions in the first month. Since then, we've raised our prices multiple times and have sold more than 1,200 descriptions in total.

After I became known as "the book description guy", I expanded into courses and coaching. I used the increased income to hire part-time contractors to help with the workload and the backend. There have been peaks and valleys with the business since, but learning the formula of hard work plus a tested good idea has set me up for a lifetime of success.

What's your advice for entrepreneurs who are still struggling?

An author's path to success may end up completely different from mine. No matter what your business, however, there's always room for hard work. There's always room for setting up a regular system for yourself and doing what others aren't willing or able to do. Sometimes you'll have to do what feels beneath you and sometimes you won't feel like doing anything at all. But if you persevere and keep pushing to give your target customers what they want, then you'll get through your own dark period too.

> To find out more about Bryan's journey, visit www.BryanCohen.com.

DEREK MURPHY: Hone Your Craft Until You're the Best

I've known Derek for years. I interviewed him for my 5-Figure Author Challenge and I regularly check his Facebook group for authors.

Derek studied fine art in Florence and philosophy in Malta, and has been featured by CNN for running writing retreats in medieval castles. Derek changes countries every month, seeking out inspiration and adventure while exploring productivity hacks and motivational strategies to avoid procrastination and create work that matters (it's a constant battle). He writes nonfiction books about creativity and young adult sci-fi and fantasy, and also supports writers with publishing tools and book marketing resources.

When did you start considering yourself financially successful as an author? How long did it take after publishing your first book? How did it feel, and why?

I straightened my jacket and entered the conference room, determined to make a good impression, but immediately knew something was wrong. Five members of the university board sat with smug smiles on one side of the long, polished table. I took a seat across from them. Between us lay a copy of my book. I was reasonably proud of it. After my first book bombed terribly, I almost quit writing for good. Instead, I went back to school, studied book design and marketing, and spent years revising it to improve the quality. I did the best I could to launch it: I reached out to reviewers, built a website, went to international book fairs, got featured on high profile blogs and websites, and even got enough visibility to sell 4,000 copies to a Russian publisher.

But after I stopped marketing, sales dropped to zero. So there I was, seeking a university teaching job that I didn't really want, but desperately needed. I'd recently sold my book collection to pay the rent. My wife was working a crappy job at the airport, selling duty-free trinkets for slave wages while I finished my literature doctorate. I felt like a failure. It was time to grow up and get a *real* job. I knew I had one ally in the room, a friend of my graduate advisor. But the other faces looked apologetic and uncomfortable, like they knew this was a waste of time, and one was outright hostile. She picked up the book flipped it over, pointing to the publishing imprint I'd created.

"This is *you* right? You *self*-published this?" Disdain dripped from her voice. My palms were sweaty and my heart started to race. My throat tightened painfully. This wasn't an interview; it was an ambush. I nodded, and I could see they'd already decided to vote against me. There was no place in their faculty for a self-publishing author. I blustered through the interview, gave the worst teaching presentation ever, and breathed a sigh of relief when it was finally over. Outside, surrounded by trees and dappled light from the setting sun, I clenched my fists and vowed I would never beg for a job again.

First, I became a professional book editor, then I used my fine arts background to start designing book covers. Although it was a struggle, within a year I was making enough money for my wife to quit her job. I wanted to figure out how to help my clients sell more books, so I learned everything I could about online sales and marketing. After designing more than a thousand book covers, and working with hundreds of best-selling authors, I was starting to get a hang of the publishing business.

I realized the biggest challenge for most authors was the marketing — it was painful to watch desperate authors spam Twitter and Facebook, begging anyone to buy or support their book. Even if I'd designed a brilliant cover, they still needed to get in front of their readers. And as I'd already discovered, having a good book with a great cover wasn't enough to ensure long-term sales. Even worse, most book marketing tactics being used were not only inauthentic and uncomfortable for authors, they didn't work at all.

In 2014, I put together *Book Marketing is Dead* to help authors market their books without resorting to spammy tactics. It has been permafree for years and is usually No.1 in several categories. (It still brings me new leads all day long with zero work or investment.) *Book Marketing is Dead* is a basic primer to doing online business, by providing value and nurturing real relationships — not sleazy marketing hacks.

But I didn't want to be one of those guys who just talks about marketing and isn't actually selling books (my specialized nonfiction books do sell but I wanted to prove that my tactics and publishing experiments worked for fiction as well.) By this time, my business had grown to the point that my wife and I could travel full-time, speaking at writing conferences around the world, but I wasn't satisfied. I wanted to be earning a living from *my own* books, instead of helping others publish theirs.

So I committed to publishing fiction. It was hard, painful, soul-wrenching and more challenging than my doctorate thesis. But I got some stuff done. Two unique strategies helped the most. First, since I had no experience writing and finishing a complete novel, I allowed myself to complete several attempts at Part 1 — half-novels that ended on cliffhangers — and publish them. Second, I made most of them perma-free for several months.

Since I had no platform for fiction, this was the easiest way to get my books in front of the right readers with zero marketing or promotion. At the same time, I invested in platforms and listbuilding. I built a site for my fiction, and a joint author site for my genre. Most authors are skeptical about blogging, especially for fiction, which made it surprisingly easy to get ahead. By creating content and lists of my favorite books for every genre I wanted to write in, and featuring other people's books instead of my own, my articles rank on the first page of Google for dozens of keyword search phrases, like these:

- ❖ Best YA vampire books
- ❖ Best YA time travel books
- ❖ Best YA mermaid books
- ❖ Best YA angel books

Secrets of Successful Authors and Publishers

I get about 500 visitors a day of highly targeted traffic, and about 50 opt-ins a day, with no marketing or advertising. Paired with a well-written autoresponder series full of interesting stories (not promotions), I can get readers to like and trust me. I offer them free books or samples, encourage them to start reading, and turn them into supportive fans. All of this is running on autopilot, so I can focus on writing books, not on marketing or promotion.

At the same time, I built a community for YA authors and after a few years, just from Facebook interaction, consider myself friends with dozens of bestselling authors in my genre. I nurture others, support other authors, and rarely ask for anything in return. I also did some non-conventional stuff — book marketing strategies that nobody else was using, like building a list of 25,000 readers with book giveaways, which gave me a reason to promote other authors' books while providing something attractive to my target audience.

Within six months I had:

- 1,000+ reviews — honest, organic reviews from readers who loved my books
- $21,000 in sales — 6 million pages read and more than 200,000 downloads
- 27,000 subscribers — eager to hear news of my next release.

In 2017, I finished five books in one year, and thanks to a featured BookBub deal and a sequel on preorder, I made $8,287 in April. I thought I'd made it… but I couldn't keep up the rigorous schedule. I missed a deadline and got my preorder privileges taken away. Without the hard deadlines, it was difficult to self-motivate, and I gradually let sales slide. I was burnt out, and even depressed. But I wasn't worried. I'd proven that I could make a living as a writer, and earn twice the salary of the average college professor.

I spent the next year improving and finishing the books I'd started, studying craft and story, and planning new series I knew would sell even better. The only problem was I couldn't focus on writing new books if I was spending all my time and money on book marketing. I realized that the only way to make a living as a writer was to write books that sell themselves, and have funnels in place to attract new readers and convert them into fans on autopilot. So I developed a totally new system to write bestsellers on purpose, remove all the fear and doubt, and get free visibility that makes book marketing unnecessary.

It's imperative that you write books readers love. "Words are our most inexhaustible supply of magic." (J.K. Rowling) Whether by pen and paper, or a laptop by the beach, writing is pure creation. Anytime, anywhere, you can bring something out of nothing, like Athena self-manifesting from Zeus's forehead, fully armed and ready to conquer the world. Writing is a magic. It's exciting, mysterious, and for that reason, sometimes impossible. After all, what do you do if the muse doesn't show up? If you're not really in control, how can you defeat procrastination? More importantly, if the universe whispered inspiration into your ear, and you're fulfilling a sacred and necessary duty to share wisdom with the world… why can't you get anyone to buy your book?

The common answer is that creativity is not about earning a living or financial gain. True art is its own reward. Common wisdom dictates you *must* write from passion, and do what you love, or else your writing will be stained with the taint of consumer interests; branded like a scarlet letter. The only problem with that ideology is that most people write books nobody wants to read. But they publish and market the books anyway, hoping for luck to overwhelm practical concerns like whether anybody wants to pay for what they've written.

Everyone loves the famous quote "What you believe, you can achieve" from Napoleon Hill's *Think and Grow Rich*. But if you've read the book, you'll know that thinking about money is only the first step. The second step is providing value. Hill says, "It is one thing to want money — everyone wants more — but it is something entirely different to be worth more. Many people mistake their wants for their just dues. Your financial requirements or wants have nothing to do with your worth. Your value is established entirely by your ability to render useful service or your capacity to induce others to render such service."

In his self-analysis questionnaire, Hill instructs us to ask ourselves these questions routinely:

- Have I delivered service of the best possible quality of which I was capable, and could I have improved any part of this service
- Have I delivered service in the greatest possible quantity of which I was capable?
- How much time have I devoted to unprofitable effort which I might have used to better advantage?
- Has the purchaser of my services been satisfied with the service I have rendered, and if not, why not?

What I've come to realize is that it is far more rewarding to create work that matters to people. It isn't *their* responsibility to support my creative habit. It is *my* job to create work of intrinsic and obvious value. This is the fundamental insight behind my blog Creativindie.

The secret of marketing, and business in general, is not convincing people to want what you have, but making things that people want or need. My success as an author came only after I decided to follow Napoleon Hill's advice and write better books, that more people would enjoy.

What have been the key factors to your success and why?

If you want to finish a book, believing your work is an inspired masterpiece of unprecedented genius may give you the confidence and enthusiasm to keep going, even when things get hard. But if you want to write and grow rich, you must follow Napoleon Hill's advice and always strive to increase both the quality and quantity of the service you provide, and focus on reader satisfaction. (For fiction, your service is the reading experience itself; for nonfiction, your service can also include inducing others to take action.)

Authors who resist the idea of providing value in equal or greater measure than the recompensation they seek usually have a few deeply-rooted ideas about creative production, so let me dig into them now.

Passion leads to quality.

This isn't true. There are many novice writers who have tremendous passion but horrible craft. Skill comes from repetition and practice. Passion will help writers persevere, even after failing for years, until they finally develop the necessary skills and also figure out how to write books readers love. People who believe this also think books written with passion are somehow better — even if (or especially if) nobody wants to read them.

Quality equals value.

Some authors think, because they care so much about their book, and spent years laboring over it, carefully choosing every single word so each sentence glows and hums, that it must be *worth more*. Not true. The time you spent, or the care you invested, does not necessarily increase the value of the work — nor will it necessarily make it more enjoyable — because passion is not transferrable. The assumption is that if you enjoyed writing it, readers will enjoy reading it. But readers don't care about your passion. If the story doesn't interest them enough to keep reading, they won't enjoy the book, even if *you* enjoyed writing it.

Value and passion cannot coexist.

The most common objection I hear from writers is that writing for money would be torture, and they physically just can't do it, even if they wanted to. Passion comes from uncertainty and fear. This is what writers are addicted to; it's the danger of the quest that makes the triumph so sweet.

Readers rarely want a completely new and foreign reading experience. They don't want to feel confused or lost. They want something satisfying that sucks them in and makes them hold their breath. They want characters they love; stakes that matter; a suspension of time and space as they turn the pages, eager to find out what happens next. If you want to create an amazing reader experience (increase value), then you must hone your craft until you're the best at what you do.

Would you rather hire an eager but inexperienced brain surgeon or mechanic, or someone so proficient they can do a perfect procedure better and faster? Writing is one of the only professions where people think if you consistently produce high-quality work that readers love — and make a living from it — you must be doing something wrong.

Wouldn't you rather get paid because readers love your books, instead of because they pity you for being a starving artist? Wouldn't you rather write books readers love, instead of books nobody enjoys? Wouldn't you rather get rave reviews and testimonials from readers, instead of negative reviews that the book was boring or they quit reading because they were bored?

If you look at those authors who are actually making a living with their writing, a very small fraction of them accidentally got lucky, because their passion happened to overlap with what resonated with readers. The others are authors who are using this exact system — to create books readers love *on purpose*. That's the first secret to making a living as a writer.

You can do it, but you have to want to.

Derek invites you to download a copy of *Guerrilla Publishing* for free on his website, www.creativindie.com/GP

MATT STONE: Treat Your Book Like Your Life's Work

I met Matt when he was still going by the name of Buck Flogging. Matt has been incredibly kind to me and we've developed a relationship in which we call one another brother and sister!

Matt started out as a passionate purist, doing extensive health and nutrition research and documenting it on his blog, with no entrepreneurial interest or knowhow whatsoever. Perhaps the unlikeliest of entrepreneurs, he actually garnered a large following online, published some books and became a multiple bestselling author at the helm of a business generating nearly $200,000 in sales annually. All of this was achieved without ever reading a single book about entrepreneurship, business, online marketing or anything of the sort.

But as his interest in health and nutrition research waned, he looked to all the lessons he'd learned from watching others in his eight-year journey online, drew upon many more lessons learned from his many successes and failures and launched a superior business with his partner Rob Archangel. It was successful in just a matter of months, and with the launch of Buck Books, which became more or less an overnight success that has gone on to make a few shockwaves in the publishing industry, it has become apparent that these repeated successes aren't luck.

He actually knows his stuff, and QuitN6 was launched to reveal the strategies, tactics and knowledge that other unlikely entrepreneurs, like himself, can use to make the leap to successful and sustainable self-employment online.

When did you start considering yourself financially successful as an author? How long did it take after you published your first book? How did it feel and why?

I actually became financially successful as an author *before* I published my first book! Before I ever published books in the traditional sense, I sold my books on my own website. First, I sold them individually, then I bundled them together, then I added audio and video in large packages that I sold for more than $100. I was able to get my site hauling in roughly $15,000 per month before I published on Amazon and other vendors, and I was able to carve out a full-time living for the first time selling books that didn't even have book covers! Just hideous, typo-filled, unformatted word documents that I saved as PDFs!

My first year after publishing a book I earned about $6,500. I did about $23,000 in Year 2. And the third year, when I finally was able to cut the cord of unwanted employment for good, my site hauled in roughly $40,000.

It was, and still is, what I consider to be the greatest achievement of my life. That moment when it sank in that I was making a successful living without having to go to work, and that being a successful author wasn't just some Tim Ferriss-induced pipedream, was absolutely surreal.

What have been the key factors to your success and why?

The key reason was persistence, and the key reason I was persistent was that I deeply enjoyed what I was doing. Never in my life had I been very productive or accomplished much. I resented work, career and all things pertaining to money. The longest I consecutively worked a full-time job (from age 16 to 33) was just nine months!

But when I pursued something I really wanted to pursue for curiosity's sake, with no goals or end point in mind, and with no intent for financial gain from the outset, I was a man on fire. I had an extreme hunger for knowledge and became downright obsessed.

In just a few years, I went from a cashier at a health food store to a well-known health and nutrition scholar specializing in metabolism and eating disorders. I was invited to speak at big conferences in front of audiences of up to 500 people.

There is actually a real science to tapping into hyperproductivity through fun. For more, I strongly recommend reading the book, *The Joy of Craft*, the work of Alfie Kohn or Daniel Pink, or my own book, *Goals Suck*. A stew of the ideas in these books can help you tap into your own maximum personal potential.

What has been your worst decision as a writer and how did you bounce back and still get to where you are today? Did this failure set you up for your current success?

My worst decision as a writer took place during my transition to getting paid! I launched my first book and a new website on January 1, 2009. I had been building up an audience on my blog for two years prior, and I thought I was a bigger deal than I really was. I launched my first book and a subscription to a paid monthly newsletter with no idea what to expect. I made around $400 on the first day, and I thought I was the king of the world! Then I made just $150 on the second day and absolutely nothing for the next 13 days. Not a single sale!

Before I launched an actual paid product I was on a mission, deeply in love with the pursuit of knowledge and the development of my expertise and skills as a thinker and educator. But when the money rolled in and I got elated, followed by the money coming to a screeching halt and feeling defeated and depressed, I lost interest for a while and began pursuing day trading! Yes, I went from a man on an amazing mission to a sleazy, slimy, self-absorbed, day-trading weasel.

Fortunately, I got greedy and began trading on the forex markets where the stakes are ludicrous (it's literally 100 times more volatile than the stock market!), and my entire life savings up to that point of around $28,000 were completely wiped out. This experience snapped me out of this absurd diversion, and brought me back on track. From that day forward, I vowed that I would never pursue such lifeless ambitions and would always stay true to my core passions and desires no matter what.

Yes, I almost gave up on my dream completely, and losing everything was the thing that saved me. I've no regrets. It was a mistake I evidently needed to make to strengthen my convictions and restore the relentless persistence it required to help me reach full-time-author status.

What has been your best decision as an author and why?

My best decision as an author came from something unrelated to being an author. Being an author was something that forced me to learn something much more powerful and lucrative than writing books. It forced me to learn how to be successful in starting up and operating businesses online.

I write very little these days (I've published just one book and two blog posts in the last 15 months!) and instead focus on overseeing my many online businesses, as well as helping others start their own. My business brings in far more money, and I only have to work 10-15 hours most weeks.

What is the best investment you've made as an author and why?

Learning how to build a large email list is probably at the top of the list. It's easier to get an email subscriber than it is to sell a book, and email subscribers are worth more to me than the one-time sale of a book! That art of writing good sales copy and great emails has been incalculably more valuable to me per word written than the words I wrote for blog posts or books over the years.

To be a very successful author, you have to become good at selling and marketing and running a business, and if you are good at those things, you'll probably make more money focusing on that than you will writing books all day!

But I still love to write books, and it will be a part of my life forever. Most of my businesses help provide services for authors, so I'm still living and breathing publishing every day.

If you were deprived of all but one of your marketing tools, which would you keep and why?

It's a bit of a coin toss between writing good sales copy and building an email list. In some ways, these work synergistically. For example, being able to create a great sales page to sell a product or service effectively is the catalyst to building a large email list quickly. If I have a $100 product and my sales page is so good that 10 percent of visitors to the site buy that product, that means I'm making $10 per visitor to my site.

I can use this large email list for a successful launch of a book on Amazon any time I want. It's being able to sell something effectively that is at the core of all my marketing.

What is an unusual habit that you have as a writer that helps you succeed?

What has helped me be successful over the years is not having any habits or a set routine. This means that I'm only working when I want to work (for the most part). And if I'm working on what I want to work on when I want to work on it, I keep the enjoyment of my work extremely high. As you already know, enjoying what I'm doing is the only thing I've ever found to make work attractive enough to do consistently!

What would you have done differently if you were to start your writing career with the knowledge you have now?

I'd learn much earlier how to be effective in building an email list. For the first five years of blogging, I got nearly 10 million visitors to my site but only built an email list of around 3,000. Once I learned how to build email lists more effectively, I got my second 3,000 subscribers in just weeks and went on to get more than 50,000 subscribers in the following year (I've since got more than 300,000!).

What bad advice do you often hear on the subject of self-publishing and book-marketing?

The worst advice I hear is "Quickly write and publish as many books as you can."

One excellent body of work, fully professionalized in every way, and given a proper launch and ongoing marketing can pay your bills for the rest of your life. Don't just assume every book is going to make only $300 per month and try to publish 100 books so you can make $30,000 per month! Instead, create a masterpiece and dedicate your life to selling it. Build an entire business around that one flagship book if you can.

I say this from the point of view of someone who has written and published a ton of short, sloppy books hastily. I've so much regret. One book in particular, *Eat for Heat*, was a raging success. But because the book was short, sloppy and poorly edited, it steadily died a painful death as average reviews have gone from 4.9 to a dismal 3.3. Meanwhile, sales have gone from around $15,000 per month to about $700. If

I hadn't had a 'rinse and repeat' mindset, I would have made millions of dollars from that book by now.

So my advice is to treat your book like your life's work. Pour lots of time, money and preparation into it. And then swing for the fences when you hit that publish button. Anything done with less love and dedication is almost certain to fail.

What do you do when you feel demotivated or overwhelmed?

I work on something. Work, when you have the right relationship with it, is the ultimate provider of fulfillment in life. I've had tough times in business to be sure, with huge ups and downs that absolutely crushed my soul. And I have indeed taken long breaks from my work to 'work' on other things, such as learn foreign languages. But I've rarely stopped using my mind actively to keep the feeling of progress going. When I have, I quickly became depressed!

If you are sitting around doing nothing, waiting to feel motivated, it may never come. If you get in touch with what you're truly interested in and love doing and start doing that with fervor and dedication, you won't need outside motivation anymore. You'll need motivation to take breaks, go outside, and go on vacation!

What's your advice for authors who are still struggling?

Work with an experienced professional. Most authors have a tendency to want to do everything themselves, or are too proud to seek the help of another. It can save you a lot of heartache and time to get help from someone who has already figured out the stuff you haven't yet!

Secrets of Successful Authors and Publishers

You can connect with Matt at his book cover design service, www.100covers.com, his book advertising agency, www.BookAds.co, or his book promotion site www.BuckBooks.net, which has sold millions of books for more than 3,000 authors since its 2014 debut to the author community.

PART 2: COMMUNICATORS

CLAIRE DIAZ-ORTIZ: I Started to See What it Meant to Have a Voice Online

I first got to know Claire when she invited me to speak at her Success Mentor Summit. When we were introduced, I learnt that she was one of the first people who got a Twitter account — so early that her handle is @claire!

Claire is a successful entrepreneur and mother of twins and more!!! I always marvel at how moms of twins find time to sleep, not to mention run a successful business!

Claire is an author, speaker and innovation advisor who was an early employee at Twitter. Named one of the 100 Most Creative People in Business by *Fast Company* and called the "woman who got the Pope on Twitter" by *Wired*, she holds an MBA and other degrees from Stanford and Oxford and has been featured widely in print and broadcast media. She's the award-winning author of eight books that have been published in more than a dozen countries.

When did you start considering yourself financially successful as an author? How long did it take after publishing your first book? How did it feel, and why?

It's interesting the way this question is worded, because it makes me think a lot of something Elizabeth Gilbert talked about in *Big Magic* — this idea that you can write one successful book, and you can even write several successful books, and yet when the blank page is staring at you and you're getting ready to write a new one, you feel all those same feelings you felt the first time you did it. You don't know if you'll be able to do it again. You certainly don't know if anyone will ever buy it. And you don't know if the world will finally figure you out as being not the person they thought you were.

One answer to that question is that I'm not there yet. And then another answer to that question is it's a series of different milestones. I remember the first book that I wrote. I had this dream of writing a book but I didn't know how to do it. To get my first agent, therefore, I asked Google how to write a book proposal and how to get an agent. That was the first step I took almost ten years ago in terms of writing my first book.

I'm sure in that moment when that agent took me on, I thought, "Wow! I've really made it." Those moments of feeling success do happen along the way and obviously the degree to which you feel it does change over time as the successes get bigger and the money gets bigger.

The key factor in terms of starting that whole journey was starting a blog. It changed everything.

What would you say have been some of the key factors to your success and why?

One of the biggest things was just understanding that having a voice wasn't enough; that if I wanted people to read my words, I had to get out there on the Internet.

That happened in 2006. I was about to go on a yearlong journey around the world. At the time, I had an amazing job as on online editor. I could work from anywhere, so I wrangled my best friend into traveling with me for a year. Within the first two weeks of our trip, we were in a tiny hostel room in Spain, and I was about to run a marathon and I hit publish on this first blog post (the blog at the time was about traveling around the world). It was a turning point, right. I didn't know if it would be anything. I thought probably in those initial days that it was just for friends and family. And then slowly it grew and slowly I started to see what it meant to have a voice in the online world.

It started then; getting my footing then has allowed me to reinvent myself a few different times in a few different blogs and to find the path to publishing books and having a voice online and a voice in print. I was lucky in that I was introduced to the online world of blogging in 2006 and also joined Twitter in 2006, so blogging and social media came early enough in the journey that I understood that it was going to be part of the writing story from the early days.

What was probably the worst decision you've made as an author and as an entrepreneur? And how did you come back from that?

There are a few different answers to this question but the answer that seems most relevant concerns something that happened in my personal life in the last few years. When I was expecting twins, I had a very difficult pregnancy and then they ended up being born premature by two months. Not only was it challenging on this personal level, I was incredibly worried about the twins' health and their lives in the first few months. At the same time, we had another major concern — my beloved father-in-law was sick and would soon die. All this was happening and I felt that I had no time to write. That is something that happens to many authors. That year, when I was so focused on my personal life, I felt that I had no time to write. And I lost touch with myself in the process.

Then I started realizing what had happened and coming to terms with it all. It was through writing that I got to find my footing again. And I tell this story in the light of a very personal experience that happened to me through one very bad year, but many of us have this experience on a day-to-day basis.

What does it mean when you don't prioritize the writing? It's a big challenge that we all face and a challenge that we all have to figure out how to overcome. We need to be writing.

What has been your best decision as an entrepreneur (writing and/or marketing) and why?

The best decision is that I came to the online world almost before I formed myself as a writer. That meant that I didn't have to drag myself out of bed in the morning to get on social media. That's something that I do see many authors facing these days. You see successful authors who are doing well but know they could be doing better and reaching more readers if they were to develop themselves a bit more online. That's always such a sad thing for me to see because I see so much lost potential there.

What do you think was the best investment that you made as an author and as an entrepreneur?

The best investment that I've made is also perhaps one of the most unusual habits that I have as an author and an entrepreneur. That is the way I write is very specific. We all have our specific idiosyncrasies in how we write things; for me, writing the first draft of a book really has to happen in some type of seclusion. What I do is this: when approaching a book project, I find a place — whether it's a hotel room or a cruise ship — to go and pound out that first draft. Every time I sign a new book deal, I know that part of that advance is going to have to go towards this time; whether it's one week or two weeks, whatever it can be, to set aside to get that first draft out. Then, once I have it, I can bring that into my regular rhythm of work. Being completely isolated during the first draft is so important. There's a very clear investment of money that has to happen to make that happen; a very clear investment of time as well. Now that I'm a mom of three, it's a lot harder for my whole family to rally around this, but it's so important because if I don't do that, the book simply does not get started on the right track. It's something that I absolutely have to do.

What would be the number one marketing tool that you would continue to hold onto?

The one marketing tool I would care about these days is my newsletter. A newsletter is simply the most effective marketing tool around. A newsletter is the way to speak directly to your readers. It goes in someone's inbox. It's the most effective way to make sure that what you are saying is being heard, is being read and is being absorbed by the people you want to influence.

What do you think you would have done differently if you knew then what you know now?

I'd have started that newsletter much sooner. I blogged for years and years before thinking about a newsletter. Some of that had to do with the way marketing changed. Had I started that newsletter earlier, I'd definitely be further along.

What do you think was some bad advice that you received at the beginning?

One of the worst pieces of advice that I received was to think more about the marketability of a book topic than about what I wanted to write about. It's important to make sure that you are passionate about what you're going to write about and that it's not all just a giant scheme to figure out what the market wants right now because that will only take you so far. I see this trend happening with a lot of authors around me who are trying to leap on the next big thing and write a new book or article about a hot topic whether or not it's a topic they feel passionate about and they want to own for the next two to three years.

Book projects are intense, life-consuming projects. Making sure that you care passionately about what you're writing about is very important.

What do you do when you feel unmotivated or overwhelmed?

The absolute best thing you can do is step away. I'm a big meditator and I listened to meditation recently on the Calm app, which is what I use. And it was a meditation all about engaging your default mode network of your brain more. And the way to engage your default mode network of your brain is basically just to chill out, and think of nothing; meditate, go for a walk, not listening to a podcast, let your brain settle, and let it not have some input for a while. For me, when I'm demotivated or overwhelmed, the answer is not to push in that moment. The answer is to step back and feel calm.

What's your advice for authors who are still struggling?

Go out and build yourself an online presence step by step, brick by brick. It doesn't have to be perfect but start building an online presence because an online presence leads to an online following, and an online following will help you when you publish your first book or your 100th book. That would be the first thing I would recommend.

The other thing would be that no matter how strapped you are in terms of the time and/or how much work you're doing, prioritize meeting, connecting and networking with other people who do the type of work you do. It's these relationships that we build along the way that can help take us from zero to a hundred, or mean we don't have to relearn something that someone else has done. Having these connections helps us get to where we're going faster.

You can connect with Claire online at her website www.clairediazortiz.com.

Of course, she's also on Twitter @Claire.

KIRSTEN OLIPHANT: I Release My Inner Simon Cowell

I've been in touch with Kirsten since I interviewed her for my summit. Kirsten has five children and still has time to write!!!

Kirsten wrote her first novel in the third grade. It was terrible. She kept writing anyway and went on to get her MFA in Fiction at the University of North Carolina at Greensboro. Her books include five nonfiction books about business and faith and two fiction books under the pen name Emma St. Clair. In 2016 and 2017, she was included in the list of the Top 25 Social Media Power Influencers in Houston.

When not writing books, she hosts the Create If Writing podcast, helping writers learn to build their online platform without being smarmy. It has been named one of the Top 23 Podcasts for Writers by *Writer's Digest*. She has spoken at events like Podcast Movement, Social Media Day Houston, BlogHer Food, Blog Elevated and Houston Social Media Breakfast.

When did you start considering yourself financially successful as an author? How long did it take after you published your first book? How did it feel and why?

When I wrote my first novel in the colored pages of a Hello Kitty notebook, I wasn't thinking about making money. (Of course, I was 9, so I rarely thought about money at all.) I wrote to tell a story; to see my handwriting fill the pages. I wanted to write a novel because I simply loved to write.

Similarly, I had exactly zero thoughts about money while getting my MFA. Our workshops focused solely on craft and storytelling. All of my professors were 'authors and'. They were authors *and* professors. Authors *and* something else. We didn't talk about it, but I had a deeply ingrained understanding that writing would never pay the bills. Not because writing couldn't be profitable, but because true writing was art. It wasn't about money.

Talking about money and writing together felt dirty. I never said aloud my secret hope to write the next great novel *and* secure a six-figure advance. It felt like a shameful desire. Financial talk was a massive departure from the world I grew up in, where writing equals art and art equals a poor man's craft. You wrote for writing's sake, not for money. So when I self-published my first book on Amazon a few years later, I wasn't concerned about the royalty checks. I felt successful watching my download numbers go up, thinking of my words in the hands of other people. That felt like enough. I loved publishing myself, without the help of a publisher or the need for a gatekeeper's okay. The independence of this was intoxicating and I wanted to do it again. And again. The royalty checks were an awesome bonus.

Had I stayed stuck thinking that writing was simply for the sake of art, I wouldn't have released my books into the world. I'd probably still be writing query letters or collecting Word documents on my computer, like some book graveyard. When I started self-publishing and thinking more about money, I took my writing more seriously, which has only helped my craft.

While I still don't base my feelings of success on the financial piece, I came to terms with the simple truth that I can make money with my writing and still consider it art. I can enjoy making money without being a sellout and without being smarmy. But I also don't tie my feelings of success directly to my paychecks. Money is fabulous and I'd love to make more of it. But the feeling of joy and success comes from the work itself and hearing from people who have read and loved my books.

What have been the key factors to your success and why?

My success rests primarily on two main things: my personal drive coupled with the amazing tools available today for authors.

As a mom of five young children, I'd never have found success without an intense drive. I give up things like Netflix and sleep. I don't hang out with friends as much (less of a sacrifice, since I'm a raving introvert). I feel compelled to transfer stories from my head to the page and then out into the world. I want to do this so badly that I cannot *not* write. The amazing array of tools available online allowed me to harness that drive. While many writers bemoan things like marketing and platform building, I love them!

Because of social media, blogs and email lists, I can connect directly with my ideal audience. That is so powerful! I'd have loved the opportunity to connect personally with my favorite authors as a child, but it was hard to find even a physical address to send fan mail. Now many authors respond within hours or days to a tweet from a fan. Through my online platform, I've the privilege of forming a relationship with my readers. I can share my books directly. I can let them tell me what they love to read. If I feel like it, I can show them what I ate for breakfast. My readers can share feedback or offer to be on my launch team. They can hit reply on my emails to them and share their own stories or ask questions. These tools allow authors to tear down the distance between writer and reader. And I'm all for that demolition!

I like to tell my email subscribers that until I'm like Taylor Swift (which is not likely), when they reply to my emails, I'll respond. This has set me apart and helped me amass raving fans.

What has been your worst decision as a writer and how did you bounce back and still get to where you are today? Did this failure set you up for your current success?

I didn't start taking myself seriously soon enough. Though I began blogging in 2005, I didn't consider blogging *real* writing. It seemed wholly separate from my end goal of being an author. In the same way, I was an early adopter on Facebook, Twitter and Pinterest, but I didn't think of them as vehicles to connect with my ideal readers. Once I realized that I could be using all those tools to help my writing career, I dug in and got serious. I already had a solid following, but more than the followers, I had an understanding of how to do things like use Pinterest to drive traffic to a blog to get people on my email list. Knowing how to use these tools (and the fact that I enjoy them) has given me an edge that has propelled me forward, even if I didn't take full advantage from the start.

What has been your best decision as an author (writing and/or marketing) and why?

That was to diversify my income streams and to focus on my email list.

I'm not so dissimilar from the professors in my MFA program who were 'authors and'. I'm an author and a speaker; an author and a course creator; an author and a coach; an author and an influencer. I know plenty of people who make a full-time income solely writing and publishing books. That's fantastic but is not my end goal. I feel fulfilled by writing books, but also by teaching and by helping other writers to find their success.

My email list has been crucial to help me with that diversification. As Facebook changes algorithms and Twitter updates policies and my website traffic fluctuates, I'm not concerned about my bottom line. My profits and growth continue to swing upward, all because of that direct line to my people and the relationships that I've built over the years right inside their inbox. Email has changed relatively little since the 1990s. If you're not putting a focus there, you are missing out on the most powerful piece of platform you can own!

What is the best investment you've made as an author and why? (could be an investment of money, time or energy)

I've never regretted investing in my email list. I've spent time learning to use email well, time and energy writing epic emails, and money to use a powerful email service provider (ConvertKit). Email always gives back to me. I see financial results, such as book sales, course sales and coaching clients. I also have personal satisfaction when people respond weekly to the emails I send. I've built up an incredibly loyal group of followers by using this simple and direct line of communication. While courses, advertising and other investments are often hard to track or have little measurable return on investment, email has always been the best bang for my buck.

If you were deprived of all but one of your marketing tools, which would you keep and why?

I wouldn't give up my Facebook group. If it hasn't been readily apparent so far, I value relationships. Being personally connected with my readers is a privilege and loyalty is a valuable currency. Facebook groups are incredibly powerful because so many people are on Facebook already, using it daily. Plus the strong arm of the algorithm has not (yet) come down on groups the way it has on Facebook pages.

When people are on my email list, they get a one-to-one relationship. If they hit reply on an email (which I encourage), they get me. We have a conversation. No one else knows about this; it's personal and private. In my Facebook group, my followers can connect with me, but also with each other. It's a fantastic way to foster a community and to continue building that relationship.

What is an unusual habit that you have as a writer that helps you succeed?

I'm not unique in writing terrible first drafts (which I call vomit versions), but my editing style is not for the faint of heart. While I believe in positive self-talk, I absolutely love editing my books with ruthless cruelty. I don't just kill my darlings, but I release my inner Simon Cowell on them. I write things like "terrible" and "This is the worst" and "NO, NO, NO, NO!" across the margins of my drafts! I delight in finding things to criticize and marking up my manuscripts with no compassion at all.

If another editor were to treat my work this way, I might crawl into a hole and die. But when I talk to myself like this, it becomes a challenge. I find it empowering. I rise up in response to my cruel inner editor, saying, "Oh, you think this is terrible? I'll show you!"

What would you have done differently if you were to start your writing career with the knowledge you have now?

When I graduated with my MFA, I was working on a novel. But I worked in a leisurely manner. I had zero children and no other job. To put this in perspective, I now have five children, three of whom are home with me most days of the week. I've written three books so far in the first few months of the year, and kept up two blogs, and maintained a podcast, and worked with clients. I squeeze a lot into very tiny margins. So when I look back to the years before I had children, the waste of my time seems criminal.

I'd love to go back and give myself a firm smack. Then tell leisurely me to use my time better and with more urgency. I'd write more books, take more risks and start using the tools that I adopted very early, like Facebook, Twitter and Pinterest, as tools toward writing success.

What bad advice do you often hear on the subject of self-publishing and book-marketing?

The worst advice that I hear is anything absolute. So-called experts constantly claim that they have the one proven strategy or the exact steps you need for fill-in-the-blank. We're told we should learn the rules of writing before breaking them. In a similar way, it's a good idea to become familiar with the best practices for self-publishing and marketing. Then you can test strategies to see what works best for you and your goals.

There are no rules — except when it comes to technical things or policies, like the cover sizes on Amazon or formatting for print books. Most advice should be taken with a grain of salt and examined in the context of your own goals, situation, type of writing and personality. Ignore the absolutes and those giving them.

What do you do when you feel demotivated or overwhelmed?

It's vitally important to notice the triggers that cause you to feel demotivated or overwhelmed. For example, when I complete any project, I'm hit with an immediate and intense depression. My sense of accomplishment is overshadowed by a crippling doubt and heaviness. I feel like my work is terrible and I should quit. Every time.

Now that I know this about myself, I try to have another project already set up so the transition from completion to starting is seamless. If I can shift the focus to starting something new, I move through this creative depression faster.

Find the areas and events that may trigger negativity and adapt as best you can. You can't always avoid those situations (or I'd never finish a book), but you may be able to prepare better or work through it faster.

What's your advice for authors who are still struggling?

For struggling writers, the antidote often depends on the struggle. I wish there was a web doctor for writer aches and pains that would give us the exact prescription we need. Sometimes we need to read the advice of others. Sometimes we need to shut out all the outside voices. Sometimes we need to take a break and create something in another genre or another creative outlet altogether. Sometimes we just need to press through. Sometimes we need to commiserate and sometimes we need someone to show us tough love.

The best thing that an author can do is find a few trusted friends in the space who understand or are willing to listen and be honest. I've a few people that I go to for encouragement when I hit the lows or to help me through a problem. Make deep connections with people who spur you on toward your goals.

Write and Grow Rich

Kirsten's site is the hub for all new blog posts, podcast episodes and where to connect — www.createifwriting.com. If you want weekly tips, news and resources related to writing and platform-building, you can sign up at www.createifwriting.com/quickfix

Or join the Facebook community
www.createifwriting.com/community

MARC GUBERTI: The More I Know, The More I Can Share

Marc until recently was a teenager and we first met when he invited me to speak at his summit, then his other summit, then his podcast.

Marc Guberti is a digital marketing expert, entrepreneur, and author. He is the host of the Breakthrough Success Podcast where he and his top level guests teach you how to take your business to the next level and achieve your breakthrough. He is a social media influencer with over 500,000 followers throughout his social media accounts. Marc has youthful fearlessness and entrepreneurial dedication mixed into one mindset which guides him through the process of creating products and writing content.

When did you start considering yourself financially successful as an author? How long did it take after you published your first book? How did it feel and why?

The combined effect of consistent book sales, but more importantly, watching as people bought my products because of my books made me realize I had achieved success. It took me about five months to publish my first book. It was a basic book listing some ways people can make money online. In total, the book was less than 40 pages, and the second book I self-published was just 18 pages, but those books got me more comfortable with hitting the publish button. As you hit the publish button on your work more often, you'll get more comfortable with writing books and sharing your work with the world.

What have been the key factors to your success and why?

The key factors to my success have been my continuous desire to boost my productivity, creating great content, learning as much as I can, and expanding my network. Boosting my productivity allows me to accomplish the same results in a shorter period of time. This gives me additional time to pursue other projects such as a book or a training course that I want to promote in an upcoming book. One of the best decisions I made for my productivity was delegating more tasks in my business. Delegating tasks like book formatting, cover design, social media management and various other tasks has opened up so much time. To this day, I continue looking for tasks that can be delegated and hiring people to address those tasks.

All of the productivity won't matter if I'm not creating great content for my audience. I don't want someone to buy one of my books, read through it and not get any value out of it. I write each book with the intention of serving my audience in a new way and providing them with something that will elevate them to the next level in their business and life. I also create a lot of free content to build trust with potential customers. To potential customers, your free content is a preview of what they'll get in your book, and you never know which free piece of content will be someone's first impression of you. Make every blog post, video, podcast episode and any other type of content count.

A big part of creating high value content is learning as much as I can about my niche. That's why I frequently read and re-read books. I re-read at least 10 books every month (just the insights I underlined the first time I read the book) and read at least five new (to me) books every month. During commutes, I'll listen to an audiobook. I also search the web for blog posts to strengthen my knowledge. The more I know about my niche, the more knowledge I can share with my audience.

Finally, one of the biggest factors to my success has been my network. This book is a testament to that. My favorite way for building a network is interviewing people for my podcast or a virtual summit. As of May 2018, I've interviewed more than 300 people for my podcast and virtual summits. Soon that number will be 1,000 and go well beyond that. One of my goals is to interview more than 10,000 people within my lifetime. Not only do I expand my network by interviewing people, but I also get to learn from them. Some of the people I interviewed shared insights that have changed my workflow or now play a critical part in my plans for future growth. If I come across something I want to learn in my niche, I can interview experts in that area to build up my knowledge all while building healthy relationships.

What has been your worst decision as a writer and how did you bounce back and still get to where you are today? Did this failure set you up for your current success?

My worst decision was lightly promoting the books I worked so hard on to finish and publish. For most of my early books, my form of promotion was publishing the book on Amazon, writing a good description, and including keywords. I assumed that people would buy my book because it was on Amazon. Eventually, I got a little better and did a free promotion to attract more readers, but I didn't have a plan to promote my books over the long term.

Identifying this weakness allowed me to set up for my current success. I published books at a lower frequency with the intention of meaningfully promoting the books I published. I did more research and interviewed people on what it takes to launch a successful book. With this knowledge, I invited people to join my book launch team. About 20 people were a part of the book launch team and that book was my most successful launch. The more successful your launch is, the more successful your next launch can be. With each launch, I see my strengths and weaknesses. Through honest reflection, I can identify the action steps that I know will result in a better launch than the last book launch.

What has been your best decision as an author and why?

My best decision was trading frequency with more meaningful promotion. In my experience and based on my interviews, a pattern emerged. Most of the top authors spent more time marketing their books than writing the content. You can see this with authors who often go on book tours around the world to talk about their book and reach new audiences. It's better to write one bestselling book every year than it is to write 10 books that each get one or two sales per month.

What is the best investment you've made as an author and why?

The best investment I made as an author was investing in ads. As of this publication, those ads are Amazon ads, but that can change in the future depending on how the market and world change. I'm getting a very high return on investment from Amazon ads and see more potential in the future.

If you were deprived of all but one of your marketing tools, which would you keep and why?

I'd keep ConvertKit. Your email list is your most important asset, and almost all of the revenue I generate is solely because of my email list. Any other marketing platform, tool or technique (i.e. social media) should have the purpose of building trust and attracting people to your email list. I can also use my books to grow my email list by initiating a free promotion and using the first page of the book to promote an offer people can get by joining my email list.

What is an unusual habit that you have as a writer that helps you succeed?

I have a side obsession with word count and words per minute (WPM). I've taken several online WPM speed tests just to see my WPM. I've passed 90 WPM for some speed tests. During the speed tests, you type words as they appear on the screen which isn't how writing a book works, but the potential to type 90 WPM means I can write several thousand words in an hour when the ideas are flowing. Optimizing myself in this area allows me to write my books quicker and this allows me to advance to the next stages (i.e. editing, proofreading, formatting, etc.) faster.

My high WPM also helps me with blog posts. It means I can provide valuable content to my audience without it taking too much time from writing my books. I could just record myself speaking the book and get the audio transcribed, but I prefer writing my books. That can change in the future, but right now, I prefer to type my books.

What would you have done differently if you were to start your writing career with the knowledge you have now?

I'd have hired assistants and coaches much earlier in the process. My virtual assistants complete a variety of tasks in my business that allow me to focus on my priorities, such as writing books and growing my brand. There are a lot of little things that need to get done, and many of them repeat over and over again. You need to delegate those types of tasks and focus on the 20 percent of your work that will yield 80 percent of the results. Hiring coaches has helped me achieve rapid growth since they have achieved what I want to achieve.

I hesitated for a few years before hiring assistants and coaches because of the monetary cost. However, holding off on assistants and coaches was a greater cost because I could have done so much more with the compounded extra time and enhanced skill set. Look for ways to save an extra 20 minutes per day because that adds up. Comparatively, virtual assistants and coaches can save you several hours each day. Think about what you would do if someone gave you an extra seven hours each day.

What bad advice do you often hear on the subject of self-publishing and book-marketing?

I'd rather use this question to clarify two sides of the production coin. Some authors believe in cranking out as many books as possible while other authors believe in nurturing one book very well, turning it into a bestseller, and then moving onto the next book. This is a gray area for beginners because they don't know what to do. Do they take more time to publish the book so they can promote the book on a larger scale, or do they crank out as many books as possible, do light promotions for each, but get residual sales from Amazon? If you are a new author, you should focus on getting your first book out and cranking out several more. Rush your first book just so it's published. It won't be your best work, but I believe that can be said for any author's first book. My first self-published book was less than 40 pages, but it gave me a foundation and a growing momentum. The moment you self-publish your first book, it becomes easier to self-publish the next book.

What do you do when you feel demotivated or overwhelmed?

I take a step back and read some of my underlined notes from some of my favorite books. That way, I can breeze through some of my favorite books and quickly put myself back into a successful frame of mind. *The Compound Effect*, *Secrets of the Millionaire Mind*, *No Excuses*, *Take the Stairs*, and *Rise and Grind* are my go-to books. I'll read random parts of these books for 2-3 minutes each and feel more motivated.

My other tactic is to listen to a positive high-beat song because I believe the music we listen to affects who we become.

What's your advice for authors who are still struggling?

If you're struggling, you're making progress. Every successful author interviewed in this book has struggled in their self-publishing career. You may already find yourself sacrificing short-term pleasures for long-term growth. As you go deeper into self-publishing, you'll make more of those sacrifices in the short-term for the long-term growth. If you believe your work ethic is lagging, understand that indulging in temporary short-term pleasures leads to long-term pain. I envisage long-term growth but also like to envision the long-term pain of indulging in short-term pleasures. We respond more to the avoidance of pain than the potential to gain by pursuing a certain goal. That's why I like to keep both visions in perspective.

Your success will come down to your work ethic and your skill set. You'll enhance your skill set as you flip through the pages of this book. However, my go-to way to strengthen my skill set in any area is to hire a coach. Search for coaches who can help you with self-publishing. Only hire a coach who has achieved a level of success that you wish to achieve.

Marc invites you to listen to his Breakthrough Success podcast. Visit his blog marcguberti.com and you can also subscribe to his YouTube channel youtube.com/MarcGuberti. On most of the social networks, he's @MarcGuberti.

SUMMER TANNHAUSER: They Want to Hear from You

Maybe pursuing authorship full time is not for you. You can still "write and grow rich" by writing contracts for your clients to sign or writing emails…like Summer.

Summer is a serial entrepreneur and online educator who teaches people to build a profitable 'simple little' business online, using their life experiences and passions. She's worked with hundreds of budding entrepreneurs through her online courses and masterminds, showing them how to leverage the power of relationship-based email marketing to increase sales. She has appeared in numerous online publications and podcasts including *Badassery*, *Inc.* and Teachble.

Before transitioning to her work online, Summer founded a local pet care business which she grew to a team of 20 employees and more than 1,000 clients. She took her extensive marketing and business knowledge from this endeavor, and her love of entrepreneurship, to help others open their own successful businesses online. Summer lives in Tennessee with her husband and three children.

When did you start considering yourself financially successful as an entrepreneur? How long did it take after you first started? How did it feel and why?

I became an entrepreneur before I even knew that was a thing. No one in my family had ever been an entrepreneur, and I'd never even considered that owning a business could be a possible career path. I started out as an elementary school teacher, and with summer and holiday vacations off work, I figured it made sense to fill my time with some way to supplement my income. Dogs had always been one of my passions, so before I knew it, I'd created a website (I'd dabbled in blogging previously and had picked up a few skills), made some flyers, and had my first pet-sitting client call me about a week later. That resulted in a scramble to get a client contract created and figure out what I needed to say during our meeting, and how to get them to sign on the dotted line. I had no idea what I was doing, and was figuring it all out along the way.

For the first three and a half years in my pet care business, I ran it as a side hustle. I was teaching during the day, and walking dogs before dawn, after dusk, and pretty much every weekend and holiday. Slowly, I learned how to hire a team of employees and take myself out of the field. It wasn't until my first daughter was born, and I decided to quit teaching, stay at home with her, and have my pet care business running in the background on about 10-20 hours of work per week, that I finally considered myself financially successful.

It finally dawned on me that I had a pretty good gig going on. I'd been able to quit my full-time job. I was living the dream that I'd had since I was a little girl to be a stay-at-home mom to my children. I was able to manage my business on just a few hours per day, which I could normally take care of during my daughter's naptime. I had the chance to work on my business, versus in it, as well as pursue other passions. And I was still bringing in a full-time income on part-time hours. Turning this business into a mostly hands-off asset allowed me to focus on being the mom I wanted to be to my children, while also developing my personal brand online through which I was able to share my expertise with other women desiring to start their own businesses.

What have been the key factors to your success and why?

The two key factors have been staying the course and staying true to myself. Way too many people give up before they even have a chance of making it. Even though my business focus has evolved and my message has changed, I've continued to show up and to share my voice. Simply by being here, I've been able to find success. More and more opportunities continue to come to me the longer I'm in business.

Secondly, I've stayed true to myself. I know the business that I want to run, and I know what my boundaries are. I don't want a big team of employees. I don't want a multi-million-dollar empire. I don't want to be 'on call' for clients throughout the day. I understand what model of business lights me up. I constantly ask myself whether I enjoy what I'm doing. And I make changes based on that self-reflection.

What has been your worst decision as an entrepreneur and how did you bounce back and still get to where you are today? Did this failure set you up for your current success?

My worst decision was to try to emulate other entrepreneurs that I looked up to, yet had completely different lifestyles, dreams and visions for their businesses compared to me. I've always wanted to be a mom that is there for her children throughout the day, first and foremost. And at different points in my entrepreneurial journey I lost track of that.

I started taking on one-to-one clients that required booking calls (which can't be done when children are at home with me). I said "Yes" to podcasts and virtual summit interviews that were booked for the evening hours after my children had gone to bed, giving me no time to reconnect with my husband. I tried to do Instagram and Facebook Lives and run challenges, and email my list, and create courses, and write blog posts, and the list went on. I was trying to do all those things.

I looked up to those mentors who seemed to be doing it all, and I couldn't figure out why I couldn't do the same. I'd forgotten that most of those women didn't have children (and if they did, they had a nanny during the day), and they had at least 8-9 hours during an average day to devote to their business. I was operating on about three hours of work per day.

There were moments when I wished that I had more time to work on my business, but ultimately, for me, living the mom life with my children was more important. I created my business to allow me to be a stay-at-home mom. So I had to re-evaluate what activities I truly wanted to be spending my time on in my business, and get really intentional as to what opportunities I said "Yes" to, and which I turned down.

This realization has allowed me to ditch the large majority of one-to-one client work, be very protective of the limited hours per day that I'm willing to do interviews and take calls, and focus in on what I actually want to be doing long term. I found that writing (and specifically writing emails) to inspire, to teach and to move my audience forward in their own lives and entrepreneurial journeys was what I was truly passionate about. Now, when I've a new business idea come up, or an opportunity presents itself, I always check in with myself as to whether it is going to support, or take away from, the lifestyle and business model I've developed. It's a great guidepost for me to use to ensure I'm on track with what I truly want.

What has been your best decision as an entrepreneur and why?

My best decision as an entrepreneur was to create a business that works for *me*, and not the other way around. Although there have been times when I strayed away from my true desires for my lifestyle, and let the influence of others sway me to do things that didn't fit into my life, in general I've intentionally created a business model that fits *me*.

Having had a local business prior to building my brand online has been very influential in my decisions as to the way I want to run my business. Based on those experiences, I've no desire to have a team of employees (just a few contractors here and there works great for me), I've no desire to serve one-to-one clients as a primary form of income, and I've no desire to force myself to engage in forms of marketing that I don't enjoy.

By setting these personal boundaries and getting very clear on what I want and what I don't, I've been able to avoid feeling resentful of my business, and to ward off burnout. Staying true to my personal ideal business model has been absolutely my best long-term business decision that continues to guide me today.

What is the best investment you've made as an entrepreneur and why? (could be an investment of money, time or energy)

My best investment was to join a yearlong mentorship in my second year of online business. After running a successful offline business for so many years previously, I struggled to see my online endeavors as 'real'.

By joining this mastermind and mentorship group I surrounded myself with other women who were doing the same thing as me. It opened my eyes to how everyone has the same mindset gremlins, the same doubts and the same insecurities no matter what level you're at in your business. It opened my eyes to how much mindset affects everything that we do.

If you were deprived of all but one of your marketing tools, which would you keep and why?

Without a doubt, my email list is the most important asset and marketing tool that I have in my business. When I do connect with my list subscribers in person or by phone call, they often mention that they feel like they already know me, and that it's like meeting a long-time friend. Why? Because they've read my emails, they've shared in my stories and they've heard my true thoughts written down.

I've recently restructured my business so that my email list, and the relationship that I'm building through regular emails, is even a larger part of my business growth plan. I rely on my email list pretty much 100 percent for launching new products, bringing in sales and connecting with clients.

What is an unusual habit that you have as an entrepreneur that helps you succeed?

I'm not sure if it's unusual since I hear a lot of entrepreneurs are early risers, but I like to start my day around 5 a.m. Once I grab my glasses and my coffee, I try to go right into some form of writing or content creation. Normally, that means working on an email, a blog post or some program or course content. My best writing comes when everyone else in the house is asleep and there is no chance of anyone interrupting me. With three young children, the morning is a prime time for that type of environment, so I try to make use of that hour or so of quiet to the fullest extent since it's one of my most creative times of the day.

What would you have done differently if you were to start your career with the knowledge you have now?

I'd dive in faster. I'd put all of my effort into building my tribe through my email list, focusing in on being their trusted advisor when it comes to one specific pain point or problem that they are having. I'd put all my focus into providing that value in a way that moves them to action. I'd not be afraid to share my knowledge and position myself as an expert and a trusted mentor to them.

Once that rapport had been built, I'd focus in on building *one* solution through *one* offer to provide my tribe a way to work with me and solve their pain-point issue. I'd constantly and consistently offer it to them because selling is service. They have a need and I have a solution. It's not helping anyone to hide it away. I'd continue to focus on that *one* offer, and really nail it to ensure it was getting the best results (and also, therefore, the best sales) possible, before moving onto anything else.

What bad advice do you often hear on the subject of your expertise?

When it comes to building a business primarily around your own expert status and offerings, and then sharing that message through email marketing, all too often people are afraid of their email lists! They think things like "Oh, no. I'll get too many unsubscribes if I do that" or "I don't want to bother people" or "I don't want to come across as too salesy."

Of course, those are all legitimate concerns but you've got to remember your purpose and the facts. The fact is that these people opt in to hear from you, which means they have raised their hand to learn more about what you offer. The people on your list joined because they have some pain or problem in their lives, and they had enough belief in you to take a chance and see if you can help them to solve it.

So, are you helping these people by not sending them anything? If you've got a message or solution that you know can impact others' lives, then it's your responsibility to share it! That means if you're using your email list as a way to grow your tribe, then you're doing your subscribers a disservice by not communicating with them. It's time to stop thinking of sending emails as an obligatory task, and instead using email as a way to develop real relationships with real people on your list that have real problems. They want to hear from you!

What do you do when you feel demotivated or overwhelmed?

When I'm stressed out, or just feel like there is too much to do, one of the first things I check in on are my habits and my mindset. Am I spending too much time mindlessly scrolling on social media, and need to take a break? Do I need to forget about it all for a day and take the children to the zoo? Do I need to spend some time focusing in on positive thoughts and visualizing the outcomes that I desire?

My next step is the strategic side where I try to mind-dump everything out into a document, and then start creating my to-do list from there. I like to focus on only one major project per week if possible, since I've limited time in my day to work, and I'd rather accomplish one thing per week, rather than get a bunch of little things started.

What's your advice for entrepreneurs who are still struggling?

My advice is to keep the concept of 'the *one* thing' as a guiding force in each part of your business strategy. What is 'the *one* thing' that you're going to offer? What do you want to be known for? When someone asks for a specific recommendation, we want you to be the person that comes to mind. That can't happen unless people know exactly what you do, and what your *one* area of expertise is.

And then here's the key: you've got to commit. You can't try something out for six months and move on. You can't launch a program once and then give it up because you didn't get the numbers you were hoping for. You can't change your primary business model from service provider to course creator to in-person speaker on a whim. It's so easy to get pulled away with the next shiny object or get lost in the multi-passionate entrepreneur 'business ADD' syndrome where you bounce from one thing to the next.

You become truly successful when you can take *one* business model, *one* idea and *one* delivery method and knock it out of the park day in and day out. Staying the course and keeping moving forward one step after the other is what makes the difference between an entrepreneur that constantly struggles and one that has developed themselves into an industry leader.

To connect with Summer, join her email list on her website www.summertannhauser.com.

PART 3: MARKETERS

AMY COLLINS: Do it Anyway

I've known of Amy for years but we connected only recently through Daniel Hall (you'll meet him soon). In a similar way to me, Amy helps authors get their books into libraries.

Amy is the President of New Shelves Books, one of the best-known book sales and marketing agencies in the United States. She's a trusted expert, speaker and recommended sales consultant for some of the largest book and library retailers and wholesalers in the publishing industry. In the last 20 years, Amy and her team have sold more than 40 million books into the bookstore, library and chain-store market for small and midsized publishers. She's a columnist for and a board member of several publishing organizations and a trusted teacher in the world of independent publishers.

What is the difference between being a writer and being an author?

I know so many talented writers. After almost 30 years in the publishing industry, I can easily remember the thousands upon thousands of talented writers that I've met in my travels and work. These writers have a way with the written word that I'll never have. They can turn a phrase and shape a sentence with such deftness that I stand in awe. But they are not authors. Even though many of them have written books, they are, by my definition, writers.

Authors are writers who have made the decision and taken the actions necessary to join the publishing industry in a very specific role. Now, there is nothing wrong with being a writer. It is a terrific way to make a nice living and a great way to spend one's time. Writers write. Professional writers write and get paid. Authors write and then work as champions for the books that they have written. (*Then* they get paid.)

Making the jump from writer to author means more than just deciding to publish a book or have it published. It means more than paying someone to turn your words into a book-shaped object. So much more. In 2003, I had my first book published by a professional publisher. In the first year, we sold a little more than 13,000 copies. It was a minor success.

But in truth, I was not an author. I was a writer. Yes, I had written the book. But I was too self-conscious and nervous about promoting myself and my book, so I didn't. I depended on the publisher to do all the work and my book never took off the way it could have if I had become an author when my book was published.

What I know now is that authors join the corporate, business, financial and marketing sides of the publishing industry and participate fully. And authors promote their work and connect with readers. Authors lean into the process no matter how uncomfortable they are and reach out to readers in the community to become part of the book's success. With my first book, I was not an author. I stayed safely behind the line of 'writer'.

With my second book, I decided that I was willing to step over that line and become an author. And what a huge difference it made! I was just as uncomfortable with the second book as I was with my first with self-promotion. I still felt nervous and afraid of what people would think. The difference? I did it anyway.

That has become the motto of my entire career — do it anyway! Once you decide to become an author, you will still dread seeing the reviews on Amazon that have fewer than five stars. Send out review copies *anyway*. You will still get nervous about what your hometown will think of you if you host a book launch party. Launch the party *anyway*. You will still worry about the money and how to afford promoting your book and advertising your book. Promote and advertise your book *anyway*. You will still dread sending out requests to journalists and bloggers to ask if they would like to interview you or review your book. Send out the requests *anyway*.

I do understand how hard these activities are for us. Our work and our words are our children. And I'm suggesting that if we want to be successful, we have to take huge risks with our children. But let me ask you what authors you can name who didn't take those risks; how many authors you can name that hide behind closed doors. The myth — and yes, it is a myth — of 'recluse writer' has been around for centuries. They don't exist. Emily Dickinson wrote letters and was active connecting with readers and the public with letters and correspondence. A collection of her letters at the Morgan Museum and recent studies crack away at the myth that she was a recluse. Yes, she retired to her home and even her room in her late thirties, but even from there, experts have proven that her room was a hub of promotional and correspondence activity. Harper Lee? She was given a great deal of money by her friends to take a year off and do nothing but write her book. Her editor submitted her book to the Pulitzer Committee and Hollywood and the rest fell into place from there. But Harper Lee *did* do interviews and did have the money to pay a team to promote her book. She didn't do it herself but the money from friends and the book's early success paid for its later success.

Being an author means that you've joined the business of publishing. And running a business takes time, focus, dedication and money. You will notice that writing requires most of those things too. The difference between writer and author is that one happens in the privacy of one's writing space and the other one happens out in the world in front of everyone.

I have a saying, "Time, money, talent. Pick any two." I'm afraid that if you want to depend just upon your talent to drive the sales and success of your book, you will be waiting a long time. Emily had the gift of time and Harper was given the gift of money. They both had talent. So do you. The question now is which other element you're going to use to drive your success.

I choose to use my time. So every day, I dedicate a small block of time to promote myself as an author. I hate every minute of it but I do it *anyway*. Nobody wishes that it was possible to become a successful author without having to 'put it out there' more than I do but I have had to learn how to promote my words and my writing despite how I feel. I've had to learn to do it *anyway*.

What has been your best decision as an author and why?

I'd have to say that it was the decision to do things that made me uncomfortable. The truth is I'm naturally a terribly lazy person. I'd rather watch TV and play with my dogs, while planning a motorcycle trip, than spend time online or on the phone promoting my books. I don't want to write the emails to bookstores and libraries. I don't want to ask for reviews. I don't want to book trips in hot climates during the summer months to stand in a room with seven people and talk about myself. But I do these things *anyway* because I don't want to be a mere author — I want to be a *successful* author.

This brings me to the other line in the sand I've had to recognize and step over. There is a difference between a talented author and a successful author. If I'm going to be honest, I'm not even a particularly talented author. I don't have the natural writing ability and the way with words that I so admire in others. Writing does not come naturally to me and it is not a talent that I possess in spades. I'm a good storyteller and I have advice to give that would change lives. But I'm not a great writer. So a lot of what I advise — and a number of my stories — is imparted through video and in person at events. But some people want and need a book, so I continue to put my stories and advice into books as well as other avenues.

Despite my limited talent as an author, I'm somewhat successful because I've adopted the practices and habits of successful authors. I wish I had taken on these habits and practices earlier in my career but it is my hope that they will help you. Here is a list of some of the things that I've learned separate the authors from successful authors.

- Successful authors spend time every day writing.
- Successful authors spend time every day promoting what they have already written.
- Successful authors ask for people's opinions.
- Successful authors take those opinions and honestly consider them, setting aside their own egos and desires.
- Successful authors spend time learning everything they can about the publishing industry.
- Successful authors immerse themselves in that industry and in the publishing community.
- Successful authors don't give up when things get unpleasant, boring or difficult.
- Successful authors read books in their genre.
- Successful authors always know what the big books in their categories are and who their authors are.

One of the things that I mentioned above that successful authors do is ask for advice. I want to add a small caveat about this valuable practice. Early on in my career, I would ask friends, family and people I knew for their feedback on my writing and on my marketing. What I had to learn the hard way was that it doesn't matter as much what people outside of the publishing community think. When asking for feedback, advice and guidance, it is far more useful to ask those in the publishing business than those outside of it.

Yes, my mother is an avid reader; she reads more than 100 books a year. But she is not the person to ask about my cover or marketing plan. Those questions are better aimed towards booksellers and librarians. They see hundreds of books a day and have the overview and the breadth of experience that I need. As much as I trust my mother, she just doesn't have the same breadth of experience.

Please be careful, therefore, about pulling friends and family or going online and asking your social media buds for their opinion. This is a business that we are working in and we need to rely upon people with professional experience when asking for input and feedback.

Are you ready to become a successful author? Then I suggest you do what I did. Make a list of everything you know you need to do. Then put the items on that list into one of two columns: willing to and want to. See, I *want* to do many things. I *wanted* to be keynoting at huge conferences where I could talk about myself. But that meant having to invest in filming costs, to book myself at lower-level conferences, and to work hard to convince conference bookers that I was a good presenter. I had to pay my own way for the first year or two to conferences and be one of five people on a panel. I *wanted* to be a speaker. But was I *willing* to do what needed to be done? Yes. I was. And two years later, I was being flown around the world to speak about publishing and how to become a successful author. But *wanting* it was not enough. I had to be *willing* to do the work and invest in the business side of my desires.

Here is a sample list of some of the things that might appear on your *want* and *willing* lists.

WILLING TO

(I'm already doing it or about to do it.)

- Send out requests to be considered for conference speaker.

- Send out emails asking reviewers to review my book.
- Call on other book publishing experts to endorse my book.
- Write articles and blogs to promote my advice and my book, *The Write Way*. (Do you see what I did there?)

WANT TO

(I won't spend the time or money to do these things right now but I want these things to happen.)

- Contact bookstores and libraries and ask them to stock my book.
- Write my next book.

How do I know what goes on the *want* list? I'm not doing it. But I put it on the want list because I know in time, I'll be *willing* to do these things. Many things on my *willing* list started on my *want* list.

> To learn more about Amy and about New Shelves Books, visit www.newshelves.com or email her at info@newshelves.com.

DEBBIE DRUM:
The Cream Rises to the Top

I've known of Debbie for a long time. She's the creator of the Book Review Targeter that I use to scout for Amazon reviewers, so I was very excited when I met her at a mastermind in Las Vegas hosted by Jesse Krieger. We even had dinner together and went to a Cirque du Soleil show!

Debbie is a full-time marketer, content creator and author. While most of the books she writes are under pen names, she sells a lot of content through digital marketplaces and videos.

When did you start considering yourself financially successful as an author? How long did it take after you published your first book? How did it feel and why?

I was working a 9-to-5 job. I could try different things without the pressure of having to make money, so I still had a full-time job. I did this for about two years. I worked my full-time job and started my marketing and publishing career at the same time. This is real entrepreneurship where you're waking up at 5 in the morning and you're not going to sleep until late because after your 9-to-5, you are working on building your business to be free from bosses and working for the man. When I started to see success in book sales and my first royalty, I probably went out and got a steak dinner that night because I realized if I can do this once, I can do it over and over and over again.

When I developed a system for publishing books, I was able to find out there were other people who had a lot of problems and who are struggling with how to publish a book. Because I knew how to publish quickly and correctly, and I was successful and making sales, I put together some information products and that's when I really started helping people. I grew my subscriber list and that's when you really find financial success when you can send out an email and blast anything you want to talk about whether it's a new product that you have, a new book that you have, a training that you have, a video that you have. You know you've got something when you have a bunch of people to who you can say, "Hey, I got this brand-new thing. Check it out." Once you have the ability to broadcast messages to many people at once, this is financial freedom and then just constantly growing from there is where you get even more financial freedom.

What have been the key factors to your success and why?

First, I always tell people the cream rises to the top. There's so much competition out there everywhere, especially on Amazon. What you need to focus on when you're putting your book together is you need your book to be of high quality. It cannot just be generic information anymore. I've published a bunch of books on generic information like how to grow an organic garden. That's not going to fly anymore. Even though those books still sell today, I would never publish those books anymore. It's important mostly because of social proof. When somebody reads your book and then they write a review, you want people to say, "Hey, this book is amazing." You don't want them to say, "I can get this information from anywhere." When you get social proof, you'll get more sales. You'll have a bestseller and you will get more exposure from Amazon. That's how the cycle works. It all starts with creating quality content. The second thing is delivering value to your marketplace and your niche. You have to care enough to give highly amazing information to your marketplace so they're going to continue to listen and continue to look out and continue to subscribe to what you are saying and what you talk about. Just think about it in your own life who you follow and why. What are the things you look for when you follow somebody? You need to prepare and get quality information out to your audience.

The third thing is finding solutions for common problems people have. When you can find a solution to a problem many people have, you have something to sell and you have something to talk about and people will listen to you. If it's a problem enough people have, you'll never go broke because you can talk about this problem for as many years as you like. When you have found this, you should be set for life.

What has been your worst decision as a writer and how did you bounce back and still get to where you are today? Did this failure set you up for your current success?

I realized one person can't be good at everything. If you try to go at something alone, then you're probably going to fail in a certain area. I realized the stuff I wasn't good at and the stuff

I was good at. Going at it alone and trying to do everything was one of the biggest mistakes I've made because it sets you back. If you make one mistake — for example, you publish a book and you publish the book to the wrong category — that could be catastrophic for sales. That mistake could be the difference between 10,000 people seeing your book and 50 people seeing your book. Category research is not something that excites. I don't do category research anymore.

I also don't do covers. What I used to do was I would say to my designer, "Okay. Have the cover look like this." Now I let the designer and the expert on covers give me some samples. Then I'll take a social poll and see which covers people like the best. Getting social proof — getting experts to do parts of the project, specifically in publishing — is something that I used not to do but that I do more and more today. This change has definitely given me more success.

For my last book, I outsourced much of what I hate doing. The stuff I'm good at is marketing and doing interviews and doing videos. The little nitty-gritty research is not for me, so I hired out and other people helped me do what I didn't want to do and what would slow me down if I were to do it myself. Realizing this fact has brought me to a very successful and happier place.

What has been your best decision as an author and why?

When I got the itch to write a book, I thought, "I have the itch. I need to sit down and I need to outline this book and even start writing it immediately." There are some people who can sit down for days and days and days and write until they're done. That's not me. I don't like this process.

I like to have a writing schedule. I also say — sometimes this isn't realistic — "Okay. If I want this book to be 30,000 words, I'll break that up into a time period." Let's say I want to finish the book in two months. I'll take that number and divide it by 60 and that will be my word count goal every day. It ends up being some days I'm just focused on the project for 20 minutes. Some days, if there's a little bit more research to be done or I'm just procrastinating, it might take more than 20 minutes, but nonetheless, the results are amazing. Just think if you sat down every day for 30 minutes, and at the end of 60 days, you had a book. That's an incredible achievement.

Breaking a project down works best for me. Having a schedule, sticking to it, doing it every single day no matter how much pain it is sometimes to sit down and write, especially if you have other stuff going on, especially if it's a weekend. I include the weekends in my time schedule because as entrepreneurs and authors, we have to work every single day for the most part until we don't want to anymore.

With this process, you know exactly when the book is going to be done. At the end of 60 days, you will have your rough draft. This doesn't mean you'll have the finished product, and I also recommend throughout those 60 days you're also doing other things to move your project forward.

What is the best investment you've made as an author and why?

In 2011, I purchased a course for $497. It was the best $497 I ever spent because this course taught me how to format a book very quickly. It taught me how to do Kindle books and print books. A lot of people have problems with formatting, and I never had a problem with it because I spent the money and I took this course and it's so easy for me. I never had to buy any fancy formatting tools. I never had to hire somebody to format for me. I knew how to do it from the beginning.

The other amazing aspect of this $497 investment was it also taught me how to publish to different platforms. My system was I would write the book and I would publish the print version. I would publish to Amazon Kindle and then I would publish to NOOK, Google Books and iBooks. Just knowing how to do the entire process has made me quite a good amount of money throughout the years because I was then able to show other people how to do this. Once you learn the process it takes less than 10 minutes and people charge thousands of dollars to help others do this.

If you were deprived of all but one of your marketing tools, which would you keep and why?

It would probably be my text-to-speech tool on my computer. Basically, what this does is you highlight the text, and the computer reads the text back to you. You can make it so it reads back to you very quickly. I actually wrote an entire book on this topic. It's called *Read Better Faster* and I call it the BuzzRead method. It's for those who are notorious for being slow readers. When I could hear something and when I could see something, it helped me learn it. It helped me process.

If I write a book, the last thing I want to do is re-read the book. That's not something I like to do with my time but with my text-to-speech tool, I can sit down and highlight my text, have the computer read the book back to me, and I can hear any mistakes I might have in my document, and I can see it and follow along with it and stay focused and stay engaged.

What is an unusual habit that you have as a writer that helps you succeed?

I'm a little bit laid back. I don't come from a background where I was taught 100 percent properly how to write. I know in my head and I know in my heart I could put something down but I'm very relaxed about it, so I don't really care if it's not 100 percent accurate in terms of the laws of writing. When I'm writing, I'll write something. Then I'll put a dash. Then I'll put another statement. At the end of the day, an editor will correct this. My style tends to be a little bit more relaxed just because that's the marketer (and person) I am.

My friends have told me, "When I read what you write, it sounds like you." That's exactly how I want it to sound and not something that's so serious and strict. I want it to come across as, "This is it. This is the information. This will help you. Follow my lead. Do the work. Get it done and it'll work for you." That is my style and it's worked from the beginning, so I'll continue doing it.

My advice to people is to be themselves. You don't have to work so hard when you can just be yourself.

What would you have done differently if you were to start your writing career with the knowledge you have now?

My strategy today is very different from when I started out. At that time, it was putting a lot of pressure on making book sales. There are people who make a lot of money selling books. But most people do not sell more than $100 worth of books in their lifetime. It's a hard truth many won't accept.

I've had thousands and thousands of dollars of book sales but that's not the only way I make income.

What I realized is Amazon is just another marketing vehicle for people to find you. Whether they find you through Amazon, whether they find you through a video, whether they find you through a podcast, whether they find you through a blog post, it's all just how they're finding you. There are people who make money just by having a book on Amazon. But even if they made zero money from the royalties from the book, they would still be making money in their business and making a lot of money in their business.

What bad advice do you often hear on the subject of self-publishing and book-marketing?

The bad advice I hear, especially today, is to publish one-off books. I got started writing one-off books. I've written books on gardening. I've written books on jealousy. I've written books on relationships. These are books I wrote under pen names. I don't sell anything else in those books. I don't even collect an email address. Sure, it makes me a little bit of passive income. But was it worth all the time and energy I put into it in the beginning? Maybe it was, maybe it wasn't.

If you're passionate about something and you're going to start a business, you're going to do videos on this topic, you're going to write series on this topic, you're going to sell products on this topic, and you're going to make a membership site on this topic, then, yes, write the book. Write many books on the same topic. Do it because it will make you more money above and beyond the royalties of selling your book.

What do you do when you feel demotivated or overwhelmed?

I take a step away. Then I make my simple to-do list. Then I say, "Hey, look. If I can do these five things today, I'll call this a successful day." I give myself a reward for doing those five things on my to-do list.

When it gets overwhelming is when you've a list of 80 things you need to get done and you're thinking, "Which one do I do first?" Just pick five. The next day, do the same thing and then you'll get back into the habit of working and staying focused and getting things done.

What's your advice for authors who are still struggling?

First, you might be spending way too much time marketing a book that's never going to sell. It's the hard truth that if you have a memoir, that doesn't mean everybody is going to want to read it, and it's going to take you a lot of time, a lot of money, a lot of effort, a lot of energy to get yourself out there for enough people to see that book, and then you have to convert those people into wanting to read your book. There are some books you just have to drop. Then move on with your life and start something new.

The second thing is you're struggling because you've written a book that doesn't have a big enough audience. It's not solving a specific problem people have, and you're not continuing to market the topic in other ways, so it's going to take a lot of effort to make more sales and make more money. If you wrote a book about skincare and then you wrote another book and then you're doing videos and you're doing blog posts and you're doing all this stuff and you've other products to sell around the same topic, this is a good time to focus on marketing your book and marketing yourself.

Another thing you're probably struggling with is you're not differentiating yourself from the other people who are in your niche. The reason why this business is great is because there's no competition. Even though you write a book and there might be other books on your topic, there's no competition because mostly people who read a book on a specific topic, especially if they need help with something, are not going to buy only one book and then call it a day and never buy a book on that topic again. They'll buy book after book after book, product after product after product after product.

You can connect with Debbie Drum at
www.debbiedrum.com/author

DEREK DOEPKER: Make Your Cause Greater than Your Comfort

I've known Derek for many years now. I interviewed him at my online summit. I had him teach at my mastermind. I've promoted his books via LibraryBub, my service where I connect indie authors with 10,000+ librarians.

I was excited to sit next to him at a dinner at Sushi Samba in Las Vegas after the mastermind I mentioned earlier. He's a very smart guy.

Derek is a former aspiring rockstar turned seven-time No.1 bestselling author in fitness and personal development. He discovered proven processes that took him from struggling author to selling more than 50,000 books. Now he shares those processes with thousands of authors through workshops, courses and retreats, empowering them to turn their passion for writing into a thriving business.

When did you start considering yourself financially successful as an author? How long did it take after you published your first book? How did it feel and why?

It was Christmas vacation with my family, and I had just launched my third book *50 Fitness Tips You Wish You Knew*. Up until that point, the most I had ever made in a single month was around $100 in royalties. As I login and see the sales stats of my new book, what I saw shocked me. I saw almost 100 sales *a day* pouring in.

By Christmas Day, my book had hit No.1 bestseller in the weight loss category. Within 11 days, I had made more than $5,400 in book sales. I had never had any breakthrough success until that point. The feelings were of extreme excitement mixed with a feeling of "It's about time." I had put three years of work into building my own business. It was paradoxically both surreal and completely expected at the same time to be finally seeing success.

As soon as I saw the success of that book, I knew my next step. It was to fulfill an intention I had set even before my book was successful. I had told myself, "When I figure this out, I'm going to show other authors what *really* works." After that, I went to work creating a training course teaching authors how they could have a bestselling book using the strategies that I had to discover through trial and error.

What have been the key factors to your success and why?

My degree is in music composition, and I can recall wanting nothing to do with the music business. It seems many creatives can have an aversion to business, sales and marketing. They'd rather focus on creative work like writing rather than selling. What helped me was developing an entrepreneurial mindset. This came out of necessity because I was broke, selling almost everything I owned to pay the bills, and needed to create some side business to pay the bills while I was valet parking. I started to see business and sales as a creative outlet. As an opportunity to solve problems, make a difference in the world, and express my artistic creativity. This led me to fall in love with business, marketing and sales.

In addition to the entrepreneurial mindset, there's one key skill I learned just prior to having my first No.1 bestselling book. It was the missing link that helped me make my breakthrough. It was the skill of influence. By learning how to influence readers to want to read my book and compel people to share the book, I was able to go from being a no-name author with barely any following to a bestselling author. This skill of influence ties into another key — collaboration. I don't see other authors as competitors, but rather as potential collaborators. The ultimate question isn't, "What can I do?" but rather "What can *we* do?" By focusing on leveraging relationships, I was able to reach a lot more people with a lot less effort.

Finally, perhaps the most important thing is I worked for a cause beyond myself. I believe my books can change the world by changing individuals' lives. Whenever I'd be overcome with self-doubt or feel like quitting, I'd remind myself of all the people who would benefit from what I have to offer with my books. When I take the focus off myself and put it on the people I'm serving, I'm no longer wrapped up in my own fears.

To get out of your comfort zone, make your cause greater than your comfort. By having the intention to teach others what I learned along the way, this gave me the confidence to experiment with crazy ideas. I know that whether or not it works, it will be useful information to share with others.

What has been your worst decision as an author and how did you bounce back and still get to where you are today? Did this failure set you up for your current success?

The most disappointing 'failure' came when I wrote a 350-page fitness book with a corresponding 18-hour video training course. I allowed people to name their own price to purchase it, and told my family and friends about it on Facebook. What I found was, while I got a lot of support in terms of comments and likes, very few people ended up buying it. I spent months pouring my heart and soul into something, only to have it feel like pulling teeth to get people to spend even a $1 on buying it. That's when I knew I had a lot more to learn to master marketing. I see it, however, as a necessary learning experience rather than a failure.

One thing that helped was selling books on Amazon. People were more likely to use and trust Amazon as a marketplace. It gave the work I offered credibility. While I still sell courses on my own platform, having print, ebook and audiobooks available on Amazon makes it easier for the people I tell about my books to purchase.

What has been your best decision as an author and why?

My first two books barely made any money, so naturally when something doesn't work, it only makes sense to quit and try something else. While the definition of insanity may be doing the same thing over and over again expecting different results, sometimes mastery takes doing the same thing over and over again to refine your results.

I didn't plan on writing a third book because my first two weren't initially successful, but I was inspired after attending a seminar by a man named Brandon Broadwater, who taught me the skills of influence and connection. It was my decision to write one more book that changed my life. My best decision was to keep going. Had I quit after my initial efforts, it would have been like quitting just a few feet from striking gold.

What is the best investment you've made as an author and why? (could be an investment of money, time or energy)

As Warren Buffett says, the best investment you can make is in yourself. Attending seminars in particular, such as the one I mentioned with Brandon Broadwater, had an especially profound effect. While online learning and books are helpful, there's something about being immersed in an environment of learning and going through exercises that drives the learning home. I don't believe I would have had the success I had if I hadn't regularly put myself into live environments of experiential learning and seeing role models in action. This is why I'm such a believer in coaching as it can facilitate a similar experience.

If you were deprived of all your marketing tools and could keep only one, which would it be and why?

The No. 1 marketing tool I would keep is my brain. It's known that many people who win the lottery end up going broke because they never learned how to manage that much money. Conversely, there are many who lost all their money, but gained it back again because they have the knowledge of how to make money. They have entrepreneurial skill sets that can never be taken from them, unless they lose their mental capacity.

Marketing tools and strategies may change as the times change. But the principles of success are evergreen. I know if I lost everything but kept the lessons I've learned so far on my journey, eventually it's probable I'd find another way to achieve success.

What is an unusual habit that you have as an author/entrepreneur that helps you succeed?

The ultimate strategy I've found for overcoming a sense of being overwhelmed, breaking through fear, and avoiding procrastination is using the 'three magic words' technique. The three magic words are "Can I just…?", followed by a micro-commitment. Whenever I'm overwhelmed by the idea of what I need to do, I'll find the smallest task I can say "Yes" to. For instance, "Can I just write one sentence?" This is so easy I'll always say "Yes" to it. Then what do you think happens? Once you've got some momentum, then motivation follows.

Momentum generates motivation. I'll often say, "Well I wrote a sentence, I might as well at least finish the paragraph." Next thing you know I've written a whole chapter. If tempted to surf Facebook, I may say, "Can I just take five minutes to work on my business first, then I can check it?" This creates a sense of accomplishment and helps keep the priorities in check when I do productive work first.

What would you have done differently if you were to start your career with the knowledge you have now?

The biggest payoffs in my business have come from relationships. Since relationships take time to build, I'd have started right off the bat forming relationships with other authors. I'd look for ways to contribute to what they're doing. I'd create cross-promotions that help multiple authors. I'd strive to do whatever I could to be of service to influential people in the marketplace.

What bad advice do you often hear on the subject of online business and marketing/authorship?

Is breathing a good idea? Most would say it is. However, breathing is a terrible thing to try to do if your head is underwater. Something essential for life could, in the wrong situation, take your life. The same thing is true with almost any piece of advice. A piece of advice that's perfect for one person in one situation could be terrible advice for another person in another situation.

If I see someone being too creative and artistic, the best advice for them might be, "Don't reinvent the wheel. Follow a proven path, and focus on giving the market what it wants." However, some creatives may rebel against that. That's because seemingly contradictory advice could be offered that's also helpful for those who aren't very creative. The advice for those stuck in modeling may be, "Don't just do what everyone else is doing. If you do, you'll be a me-too author. You need to find what makes you unique and different." Both of these seemingly contradictory pieces of advice could be helpful or harmful for different situations. So the worst advice is any advice that's not right for you and your situation. Learn to see everything as a partial truth.

Take the advice "Write what you love and the money will follow". There are some who will claim this is true, while others say "I tried that and it didn't work". It's obvious that if someone writes what they love but don't share it with anyone, it's not going to go very far. You need to realize that no one can give you all the caveats. You need to take responsibility for your own learning. You need to filter anything you hear and ask, "Is this relevant for me, my goals, and at this time in my process?" You also need to ask, "What else is there in addition to this?" I suggest asking, "Who has the results I want, and started in a situation similar to mine?" In other words, find good role models who've built the business you want to build from a *similar* place you're starting at. Otherwise, you could follow the great advice of one expert, only to find it's not going to be ideal for you. Then the flip-side of that is, don't just do what your role models do. You also need to pave your own path.

A good coach can help draw out your own answers to uncover what's ideal for you so you're not going too far off to either extreme.

What do you do when you feel demotivated or overwhelmed?

Since I'm heavily driven by service and intellectual challenge, there are two things that greatly motivate me. The first is seeing what I'm doing as an opportunity to help others. Thinking about how my books are going to change peoples' lives gives me more motivation to take action. What can be even more motivating though is taking frustrations and turning them into a game or experiment. If something isn't working, I get curious. I tell myself there must be a way, and then it's like a puzzle to solve.

I sometimes get frustrated when readers don't get the value of what I'm offering. Then, however, I turn it around and think, "Okay, what's another angle I can take? What if this is like a game and I gotta come up with the winning play?" Now it becomes more fun rather than frustrating.

For when I'm feeling overwhelmed, it comes back to focusing on one key thing that can move me forward, and then asking the "Can I just...?" question to take one step forward.

What's your advice for entrepreneurs who are still struggling?

There's no failure, only feedback. It sounds like a platitude of positive thinking but it's extremely practical. My first 350-page book barely sold. A lot of what I wrote in that book, however, became the foundation for a later book that went on to become a No.1 bestseller. It wasn't a waste of time, money or energy because the failed project was an ingredient later used in a successful project. This isn't just intellectually reframing failure as being necessary for success; it's tangibly repurposing failure into something successful.

The three years and thousands of dollars I spent on 'failed' efforts were an educational process. I look back and think, "I spent four years and tens of thousands of dollars on a college education without nearly the same payoff as learning to become a bestselling author." So if you see the value of a college education, consider your initial writing and business efforts as an educational investment.

You won't have the fear of failure if you value lessons more than successes. You don't get stronger when you're lifting weights, you get weaker. Only in the recovery process do you get stronger. In the same way, struggle is a setup for growth when you overcome it and get the lessons as you recover from it. Every setback, when you get the lesson, is actually setting you up for greater success down the road.

Derek invites you to download a free copy of *Why Authors Fail* at www.BestsellerSecrets.com and send me an email with your biggest takeaway and challenge to derek@BestsellerSecrets.com.

SUSAN FRIEDMANN: Out Pops Your Bonny Baby Book

I first met Susan when she invited me to speak on her podcast, Book Marketing Mentors, and I was in admiration of her royal way of speaking!

Susan is an internationally recognized niche marketing expert and 'how to' coach with a British accent.

As the owner of Aviva Publishing, she's dedicated to working with nonfiction authors serious about becoming recognized authorities in a niche market. She helps them find and penetrate the right target audience to deliver their message.

She's the host of the weekly podcast Book Marketing Mentors, bestselling author of multiple books, including *Meeting & Event Planning for Dummies* and *Riches in Niches: how to make it BIG in a small market*, and creator of the new CPR Formula training program that helps authors breathe new life into their book.

When did you start considering yourself financially successful as an entrepreneur? How long did it take after you published your first piece of content? How did it feel and why?

Early on in my career, one of my first mentors shared a piece of wisdom that stays at the forefront of my memory. It's a good reminder whenever those 'not good enough' feeling gremlins slither unnoticed into my head. Good old Bill's steadfast mantra went like this, "It takes 15 years to become an overnight success"!

It took 10 years before my first significant prospect picked up the phone, called and promptly hired me at a premium rate, all based on a word-of-mouth referral. Can you imagine the smile from ear to ear as I put down the phone? What was also unbelievable was how I just averted the arduous game of submitting the lengthy proposal. You know the kind. It often takes weeks or even months before the prospect decides on its fate.

After 24 hours of surprise success-reveling, I knew there was no room for complacency. I had to continue my marketing efforts to ensure this unexpected win turned into a more regular occurrence.

A year into my entrepreneurial quest conducting training programs for trade show exhibitors, I carried out a mission that took all the guts I could muster. It was something that certainly didn't come naturally. I asked for help and advice.

Can you imagine the courage it took to approach one of the speaking superstars in the National Speakers Association? He gave me five minutes to ask for a pearl of wisdom to kick start my speaking and training success. Plain and simple he said, "Write a book." The more I tried to resist his recommendation, the more I just needed to do it.

Over the years I've learned that there's no shame in seeking guidance from experts. The more you do it, the more it becomes easier and effortless. So, armed with this expert guidance, I needed to find a publisher who matched my down-to-earth writing style of practical tips and techniques. Crisp Publications published a series of business books that took 50 minutes to read cover to cover. A perfect match! However, the publisher thought differently.

Three proposal rejections later, and the third year in business, *Exhibiting at Tradeshows: tips and techniques for success* made its debut on the bookstore shelves.

You probably know the incredible feelings of pride and joy when you achieve something significant. It's like giving birth. You go through the gestation period. You experience the pain and anguish of the birthing process. Then, finally, after pushing, more pushing and still more pushing, out pops your bonny baby book. In an instant, the excruciating torture melts away and is replaced by excitement, love, passion and hundreds of other indescribable feelings.

The feeling of pride reached its peak when I found my book in the business section of the local Borders store. Have you ever wanted to scream for joy? I wanted to tell everyone in the store about the book. I had achieved the first major milestone in my niche market. One of my speaker/author colleagues once told me that whenever you visit a bookstore and find your book on the shelf, pull it out and display it with the front cover facing forward instead of the spine. This helps ensure passersby notice it, pick it up, look at it and then, hopefully, buy it. So, guess what I did? I followed his example and made it a practice repeating this system at every bookstore I visited that stocked the book. If they didn't have it on the shelf, I ordered it.

What have been the key factors to your success and why?

Perseverance. In other words, never give up. No matter how many times you get bopped or knocked down. Do you know about those inflatable power bags with a weighted bottom, that when knocked down, bounce right back up again? That's how you need to react. Anytime someone or something bowls you over, spring back into action as quickly as possible. I've lost count of the number of pity parties, and times I've given myself a pep talk on the importance of getting up and trying again.

Don't fear making mistakes because the more you try to resist making them, the more likely they are to happen. Your business is like a roller coaster ride with inevitable ups and downs.

However, when you set your mind to the success position, you move forward no matter what happens. Even if you think you'll never survive a situation, take to heart the words of Stephen Covey: "You are not a product of your circumstances but a product of your decisions."

It's those precise words that helped pave the way to start my training business after being downsized from not one, not two, but three companies over the course of a six-year period. Although I was devastated by the first layoff, to the point of losing all self-worth, by the third time, I knew the universe was playing a sick joke on me.

This meant that I needed to rethink what I most wanted in life. It was like getting a whack on the side of my head. It became crystal clear in my mind that helping people with their own success was my commitment and passion.

What has been your worst decision as an entrepreneur and how did you bounce back and still get to where you are today?

Getting sidetracked into various direct marketing operations shifted my focus big time. I was lured in by false 'get rich quick' claims. Only after several failed attempts did I realize that I needed to refocus and remind myself of my purpose. And that is to focus on helping nonfiction authors find the right audience to become a recognized expert. That's what motivates me to get out of bed every morning.

Did this failure set you up for your current success?

To answer this question, I'll share a story to highlight the importance of a famous quote by my guru, Winnie the Pooh, "You're braver than you believe, stronger than you seem and smarter than you think."

It was January 2002 at the National Speakers Association Winter Workshop in Hawaii. After calling my home office for messages, I learned a devastating and soul-destroying piece of news.

My publisher, IDG, decided to put my book, *Meeting & Event Planning for Dummies*, on indefinite hold just when it was about to go to press. Because of the 9/11 attacks, and the aftermath reactions, pundits in their wisdom believed meetings and events were dead and the book, therefore, redundant.

Once I managed to get my anger and frustration under some semblance of control — in other words, once I'd stopped crying and feeling sorry for myself — I set out to ascertain what I could do to rectify the situation. Surrounded by other authors, I sought their advice and counsel. Two concrete options developed — to rewrite and self-publish or wait 18 months until the publisher's copyright reverted to me. Since neither were attractive options, I decided to take on Goliath and prove them wrong.

Over the next several months, I set about researching the meetings and event industry to gather facts and figures to prove my case — that the industry was alive and well and would flourish for many more years. In the process, I found an advocate at IDG, who coached me as to the best approach. She agreed to be my mouthpiece to the sales team, the people that I had to convince with my argument to move forward with the book.

Nine months later the book was published. Since then, it's been translated into several languages and is used as a text book at several colleges that teach meeting and event management. And for the past 15 years, I've received some juicy royalties. The moral of this story is never give up because Goliaths are slayable!

What has been your best decision as an entrepreneur and why?

Being a published author is by far the best decision and the best marketing tool available. It set me up as a recognized expert in the eyes of my target market. It built and continues to build credibility and opens doors that could stay tightly locked without a publication.

For example, one of my clients, who wrote an article on weight loss, then turned that article into a chapter in an anthology similar to this one. She started marketing herself as a published author and was hired to speak by a conference organizer who had turned her down multiple times prior to being published. She's now written her own book and carved a niche in a small but lucrative section of the overcrowded weight-loss market.

What is the best investment you've made as an entrepreneur and why?

The best investment I've made and continue to make is to be a perpetual student. I love learning from the treasure trove of incredible experts who generously share their information.

I invest in courses and coaching. In the same way authors gain from my expertise, I value learning from gurus in the business. Every week I have the honor of hosting an expert on my weekly podcast, Book Marketing Mentors.

If you were deprived of all but one of your marketing tools, which would you keep and why?

The best ever marketing tool is already in your possession. It's you. In my case, it's the use of my voice to speak and train. I've built credibility as a thought leader and recognized expert with multiple publications, but the more I speak and train, the more money I make. And since we're in business to make money, you probably agree, this is a serious benefit. As long as there are audiences out there to speak to, then I know all's good with the world.

What is an unusual habit that you have as an entrepreneur that helps you succeed?

Rather than an unusual habit, I consider singing second alto in an 80-person choir as the most therapeutic activity to rest and rejuvenate my brain. We practice every Monday night and sing two main concerts every year, which draw close to 500 people each. When I focus on singing, there is absolutely no room in my mind to think about or worry about any business activity. It's like trying to cry and smile at the same time. You can only focus on one thing. This weekly head cleansing therapy allows me to come back to business with batteries charged ready for action.

What would you have done differently if you were to start your career with the knowledge you have now?

If I were to start over, it would be so much easier. The main differences include asking for help sooner and allowing myself not to be perfect.

As a child, I was taught to figure things out for myself. That ingrained habit carried over into my business career. I always felt that it showed weakness to ask for help. That, lumped together with the need to achieve perfection, caused weeks and often months of procrastination and self-sabotage. As a result, it took longer to achieve real success than needed.

Today, with so much to learn, asking and often paying for help and guidance is expected. Instead of showing weakness, it shows wisdom to realize you can't go it alone. You need assistance to move forward. Now, instead of plowing unnecessary energy into my blunders, I just laugh, learn from my mistakes and move on.

What bad advice do you often hear on the subject of online business and marketing?

"If I can do it, you can too. It's so easy!"

Yes, it might well be easy for the person trying to sell you their all-singing, all-dancing shiny object. However often they say this, they forget to mention, for example, their background knowledge and experience, as well as their own learning curve. You probably know that when you've done something for many years, it becomes second nature. It's easy, and perhaps convenient, to forget the number of years it took to achieve this level of ease. Because everyone learns differently, and has experienced different life skills, it's often a heck of a lot easier for some than others.

What do you do when you feel demotivated or overwhelmed?

I allow a day to wallow and vegetate. Then it's time to get tough on myself. Even though quitting might look like an attractive option at that moment, it's time to simplify and take stock of what's going on. Is the urgent busy work taking precedence over the important productive and money-making projects? Are different skills required to move forward? What was the last thing that worked that I can do again, but better?

It also means dealing with the head trash — those internal voices that play havoc when you're at a low point.

However, remember not to beat yourself up, especially when you think you're not where you're supposed to be. Instead, forgive yourself, be grateful and start from where you are.

What's your advice for entrepreneurs who are still struggling?

This is the time to challenge your commitment and check if you've identified why you're doing what you're doing. What's your passion? What's your message? Who's your market?

Having coached hundreds of authors over the years, the two most common mistakes I see them make are a lack of clarity, and failure to invest time and money into marketing. According to my colleague and mentor, Danny Iny, "If you don't make time for marketing, pretty soon you'll have plenty of time for marketing!"

Resolve to invest the time and money to seek out the right help and guidance to move forward on your success journey.

If you're a nonfiction author serious about becoming a recognized expert in a niche market, or you want to use Susan's unique CPR Formula to breathe new life into your nonfiction book so that you can sell more books, email susan@richesinniches.com and she will send you a step-by-step guide to her winning formula.

PART 4: TEACHERS

ALINKA RUTKOWSKA:
Like an Army Tank

If this is your first encounter with me, I'll give you a little background so that you can put my replies in context. I wrote my first book in 2010 and its success encouraged me to leave my corporate job and spend my days traveling the world and writing.

In 2014, I officially started helping authors by creating a Facebook group and sharing my marketing strategies. It became so popular that it later got acquired by another company.

At the same time, I understood the power of list building, so I started asking my Facebook members to sign up to my list before they got admitted to the group.

In 2015, I published my award-winning guide *How I Sold 80,000 Books*, which immediately positioned me as an expert in the field. Since then, I've run the 5-Figure Author Challenge, created the Author Remake Podcast, a home-study course and a mastermind. I'm also the founder of Library-Bub, where I connect independent authors with more than 10,000 libraries.

I've spoken at numerous summits and conferences, including ALLI. I've been featured in numerous publications, including IBPA. I was named most creative book marketer at the Publishing Success Summit. I've helped *USA Today* bestselling authors, CEOs and movie stars with their book marketing.

Now that I look at it, it does look quite impressive, but I want to remind you that it all started with a dream. Mix it with persistence and you're up to great things!

So, relax now, grab a cup of your favorite beverage and shoot those questions!

When did you start considering yourself financially successful as an author? How long did it take after you first started? How did it feel and why?

Almost immediately. This is not your typical answer but a few months after I published my very first book in 2010 it was gradually bringing in the same amount in royalties as my salary in the headquarters of a multinational company.

That success encouraged me to leave the corporate world and pursue my love for writing. I didn't know it at the time (and sometimes it's that ignorance that drives us to success) but you can't really expect to live comfortably off the sales of just one book.

As I published more and more books, I naturally shared my book marketing strategies with other authors. The demand for this specialized knowledge was so great that it became a business of its own and now I'm best known as a book marketing expert.

When I was in my early twenties, I had a dream to make a certain amount every month. It was about ten times as much as I was making in my very first job in the corporate world. When I hit that goal ten years later, I felt like I was walking on sunshine.

But here's the thing. You always want more. You never stop. And that eagerness, that desire to grow, to achieve more and more, that's what makes life so exhilarating.

Now I have new goals. And once I reach them, I'll have others. It never ends.

And it's the same for you. Whether your goal is to replace your day job with your book royalties, add a nice bonus to your pension or start an online business before you get out of school, it's all at your fingertips.

This book and the resources that come with it have the power to contribute greatly to you achieving your goals.

What have been the key factors to your success and why?

I recently wrote a book called *Supreme Leadership* in which I interviewed 34 CEOs celebrating 25 years in business. I asked them this exact question. Their answers varied but I divided them into six categories. They are passion, vision, persistence, adaptability, customer centeredness and relationships.

Passion and persistence are the factors that allowed me to achieve my goals. I love what I do. I love writing books. I love marketing. I love creating launch teams and preparing books for publication. I love sharing my knowledge with authors.

Sometimes I wonder what I would do if I had lived a hundred years ago. What would I do without Internet and the ability to publish any piece of content as I please? I think I'd be a teacher. I've a passion for teaching. I love running my author mastermind. I love doing one-on-one coaching. That's passion.

Then comes persistence. When I was at school, my dad used to joke that I was like an army tank. If I had a goal, I'd just keep going in that direction and nothing would cause me to deviate. It stuck. I'm very persistent but I also adapt. Let's say you want to publish your book traditionally, so you're very persistent and you pitch to hundreds or thousands of agents. But nothing happens. You, therefore, choose to adapt and you self-publish. Now you achieve your goal of publishing your book although you adapted to do that. It's important to realize when to adapt within your being persistent.

What has been your worst decision as an author and how did you bounce back and still get to where you are today? Did this failure set you up for your current success?

You will laugh when you hear this but back in 2010, after I published my very first book, I was approached by a company called World Progress Report which said my book would make a great informercial. As a first-time author, I was very tickled and my guard was down. They said there would be an interview process and if it went well, my book would be featured. After the interview, I got the exhilarating news that I was chosen for the infomercial and all I had to do was pay a "small" production fee of around $20,000.

They promised the infomercial would be featured on major TV networks. I went to the bank and got a loan. I told them I expected to pay it back immediately after the informercial aired as it would undoubtedly make me a millionaire.

Yeah, right. You know the rest of the story. Major scam.

If you have $20,000 or even $2,000 that you want to invest in your book marketing, get a great editor, a stunning cover design, have a copywriter do your book description and create a launch team to launch with a bang. Drive traffic to your Amazon page and to your landing page. Get yourself speaking gigs and guest posts.

Learn from my mistake.

What has been your best decision as an author and why?

My best decision was not to do everything myself. At first, I didn't want to invest in any type of help because I thought I could do everything myself. Well, even if you *can*, it doesn't make sense to do so.

Take creating a launch team. Yes, I can spend eight hours every day scouting for reviewers but it makes much more sense for me to train an assistant to do that. That allows me to free my mind of the petty tasks and think about the big picture.

Every author needs a partner to help them with their book marketing. A virtual assistant makes for a great partner. I'm currently working with five.

What is the best investment you've made as an author and why?

I hired a coach around a year ago. It cost way more than I ever imagined spending on coaching but the return on investment was… well, you tell me…

If every time you spent 5, you made 100. Would that be worth it?

You bet!

If you were deprived of all your marketing tools and could only keep one, which would it be and why?

My email list — big time! My list of subscribers is my biggest asset.

Whenever I launch a book and need reviews, the first people I reach out to are my subscribers. Whenever I roll out a new book or offer, I email my subscribers.

It's key to engage with your readers and provide them with quality content on a regular basis, so that they are always eager to hear from you, including when you have something for sale. This is a two-part process. First is lead generation (getting people to sign up to your mailing list). Then comes lead conversion (getting people to take you up on your offer) and you do that by regularly engaging with them.

I'm a dedicated student of copy-writing and direct response. This gives me a huge leverage with my list.

By working with affiliates and appearing on various leader boards during launches, I noticed that often people who have a list four times the size of mine don't get the results I get. Why? It's because I regularly provide value to my subscribers. Even if someone on my list never buys anything, they will still gain massive knowledge. I've a high open-and-click-through rate because my subscribers know they can expect the best from me.

Ideally, you hone your offers and your copy-writing to a point where you know how much each subscriber is worth to you. You know their lifetime value. Let's assume that a subscriber's lifetime with you is five years. Then let's say you've calculated that a subscriber is worth $60 (they will buy $60 worth of your products or services). That means you can expect a dollar a month from each subscriber. Let's say you build your list to 10,000, 20,000 or more. You do the math.

What is an unusual habit you have as an author that helps you succeed?

I'm very organized, so when I have a goal, I make sure I divide it into manageable chunks.

Let's say I decided to write a 50,000-word novel in a month. The first thing I'd do is figure out how many words a day I need to write to make that happen. Then I'd make sure I hit that word count.

Let's say I want to launch with 100 reviews. From experience, I know that to do that, you need three times more people committed to help you. That makes 300, so I'll make sure I get 300 people on my launch team. From experience, I know that I need to reach out to around 1,000 people to get 300 on my launch team.

Then I'd see how much time it would take my assistant to do it. Let's say she reached out to 50 reviewers every day. That would mean 20 days of my assistant's work.

And there you have it, a big goal divided into doable chunks.

What would you have done differently if you were to start your career with the knowledge you have now?

You bet I would never have fallen for that infomercial scam! Other than that, I would have looked for a lucrative niche first and then written a book for that segment. What first-time authors almost always do is write a book that comes from their heart (hey, that's how I got started too). It might be a family story or a bedtime story they wrote for their grandchildren. Then they publish. And nobody buys. The problem with this approach is that no marketing research has been done to justify the creation of that product (book) in the first place.

Think about multinational companies. Before they bring anything to market, they do extensive market research. As authors we should do the same. And it's never been easier. Amazon shows you exactly which categories are hot and which are not popular at all.

So first find a niche that you're passionate about where there's enough demand for your writing to be lucrative and then write.

What bad advice do you often hear on the subject of authorship?

"Do all the marketing you can". Let me explain. I'm a huge proponent of the Pareto principle, which states that 80 percent of your results come from 20 percent of your efforts. For example, 20 percent of a company's employees bring 80 percent of the revenue. 20 percent of your books bring 80 percent of your royalties. 20 percent of your marketing efforts bring 80 percent of your revenue.

Instead of doing everything you possibly can marketing-wise all the time, do many different things and quickly figure out what your 20 percent is. I know that my 20 percent in terms of lead generation is other authors recommending my stuff to their audiences. Don't get me wrong, I still have other forms of getting subscribers on my list — a permanently-free book with a link back to my website, a podcast, giveaways, ads — but those bring in 20 percent of my subscribers. That's why partnering with other authors is crucial to my business. If you look at my revenue, again the easiest way for me to get it and the most effective one is to email my audience about my offers.

Figure out what really works for you. It could be the same things that work for me, or maybe not. You will be able to pick more than 20 authors' minds in this book, so there's a lot of things you can replicate that they are already doing successfully. Don't do everything. Focus on what works for you.

What do you do when you feel demotivated or overwhelmed?

I became very aware that my occasional moments of feeling down are the reason why my periods of bliss are so powerful. It's like if you don't eat a bad takeaway every now and then, you don't appreciate the delicious food you usually have access to as much.

You know, I noticed an interesting phenomenon. You can't banish bad feeling thoughts by telling them to go away. That gives them even more strength because you're thinking about them!

The only way to get rid of thoughts that make you feel demotivated or overwhelmed is by deliberately thinking thoughts that make you feel good. And you have the power to do it! You *choose* your thoughts. Then those thoughts become thought patterns, which become habits, which become *you*.

So, let's say you had a bad day, or a bad moment, you feel 'blah'. Let's say you got a bad review for your book and you're torn apart. Instead of posting about it on social media and looking at it all the time, giving it more strength, start thinking, "That person's review is nasty and unfair but hey, at least they read the book. And if they read the book, and they're obviously not part of my fan base, then that means that I'm reaching more and more people. As an author, I've the potential of reaching millions (and I wonder what that reviewer ever accomplished!). Yes, I'm an author. That brings a certain weight to it. I think I'll add 'author' to my email signature now. Wow! It's so great I'm living in these times when it's never been easier to publish (even if it's a nasty review, but that's just part of the package). I'm an author! I'm an influencer! I'm in people's minds as they read my books! Wow!"

What did you just do? In seconds, you thought yourself out of a demotivating thought to a positive thought! That's power!

What's your advice for authors who are still struggling?

You don't drown when you're thrown into the water. You drown when you stop swimming, so keep swimming!

If you're not getting the results you expect, first look at your niche. Are you in a popular category? Is there demand for your books? If not, write something that there is demand for. If there is demand for what you're writing, which books do you aspire to compete with?

What do their covers looks like? What are their descriptions? Emulate their success. How does your book stand out? Highlight that. Then drive traffic to your book and create more books or offers to build your author business around it.

Rome wasn't built in a day. Just as your book wasn't written in one afternoon, your results won't come overnight. But if you're passionate about what you do and you keep at it, you'll get to your destination. Guaranteed.

Head over to authorremake.com and sign up for my free class on the No.1 mistake authors make — you don't want it to stand in the way to your author success!

DONNA KOZIK: Teach and the Money Will Follow

When I met Donna, I was impressed with how smoothly she ran webinars and always knew what to say. She introduced me to the term of having a book as a 'big business card', which I love.

Since we met we've had countless lunches onboard the cruise ship I often sail on and we always leave with our notebooks full of ideas!

Donna grew up on a 200-acre dairy farm in northwestern Pennsylvania and now lives near the freeways and beaches of San Diego, where she shows coaches, entrepreneurs and others how to become published authors the "fast and easy way".

In fact, she has set a personal goal of turning 1,000 people into published authors in the next 12 months.

Her system for doing this is live and virtual "Write a Book in a Weekend" events, featuring Donna's 'fill-in-the-pages' book templates plus a weekend of live audio and recorded video messages that motivate and inspire soon-to-be authors to complete their books in two days.

When did you start considering yourself financially successful as an author? How long did it take after publishing your first book? How did it feel, and why?

Someone once said, "At first they will ask why you're doing it. Later they'll ask how you did it."

I was a freelance copywriter, and my income rose and dipped wildly, spending more time in the dips than I would have liked. I remember one time I was at the neighborhood grocery store counting the cans of cat food that would feed my felines until Monday when I hoped and prayed the next check would come in. It was a scary moment at a scary time.

At the same time, I was always looking for ideas to channel my entrepreneurial spirit. The idea of having an online business really struck me as being fun and lucrative. I saw what Ali Brown, the 'Ezine Queen', and others were doing with websites, emails and information products and thought, "I could do that." After moving from Erie, Pennsylvania to San Diego, California, I co-authored a book with my best bud, Tara, who also made the trek out west (to Las Vegas, Nevada). When people found out I had written a book, they usually said something like, "I'd like to write a book someday. How did you do it?"

I got the question so often it was a no-brainer to make writing a book my area of online expertise. Then my first client, Peter Wallin, told me he was writing his book as a big 'business card'. Another light bulb went off. I could show people how to write a book to use as a kick-butt marketing tool. My branding was set. What did I need to do next to make this idea a reality?

I knew there was only so much I could do on my own; it was time to hire a coach. I wanted to know how the 'behind the scenes' operation worked. My coach told me to create a signature system — in other words, a process I could sell that would show people how to get their 'big business card' done. Got it.

I started with "My Book Writing Blueprint" — a binder, worksheets and CDs to show people how to write a book. I launched it to my email list with bated breath, expecting big sales that brought my genius into your home. And nothing. I bought a sponsor table at a Los Angeles marketing event bringing a friend with me to help handle the sales. And nothing. Back to the drawing board, with a cash flow that was dwindling fast.

I was plugging along with my online business and conducting teleseminars. The problem was no one was showing up. I asked my coach what I could do, and he asked me if I had invited people from Facebook. Now, this was when Facebook was just getting started, and you had two choices: your personal page and groups. Most people spent time gaining friends and connections from their personal page. I told him I'd invited my friends. That wasn't what he had in mind. He told me to start a group so people can say they are interested in writing a book and you can invite them.

"So, what should I call it?"

"I don't know. Call it the 'Write a Book in a Weekend Club' or something."

I hopped off the phone and went right to Facebook and started my group.

I thought it would just be a "cool and groovy study hall" for people who wanted to write a book. I didn't think that anyone would take me literally. But someone did. She messaged me and said, "Donna, I'm ready to write my book this weekend. What do I do?" Hmm. She really wants to write a book in a weekend. What would I have her do? My mind went to work. For starters, I wouldn't ask her to write *War and Peace* in a weekend — it would have to be short, maybe 60 or 100 pages. And she'd do it from her home since writing is an intimate experience — it would be hard to do in a big hotel conference room. Next, I'd share some of the 'mysteries' surrounding writing and publishing. What you needed to know regarding copyright and how to write the blurb about the author. Then I had my 'shower idea'. You know what would make this really great? If I had fill-in-the-pages templates. You just put your content in them, upload and go!

I had the idea fleshed out. I just had to sell it. That's right — this was another gem from my coach. Sell first, create second. I set the weekend dates: September 13-14, 2008. I went to work creating a sales page and setting up a way for people to pay. I created a schedule for the weekend. I started emailing my small audience letting them know what was coming. I let a few friends and colleagues know. I had calls scheduled to describe the program, inviting people to sign up. I pressed the start button.

And I made more than $7,000. As you can imagine, I was almost giddy with relief. I had something here. But I really didn't yet because remember, I was so busy selling that I didn't create anything. So, Friday night, about 12 hours prior to my Write a Book in a Weekend kickoff call, I started putting the course together. I outlined what I would say on the calls and created the fill-in-the-pages templates for people to choose from. I made and sent 'call reminder' emails on the fly — and I had a ton of fun with more than 70 people taking part!

Two weeks later, I received a package in the mail from one of my first graduates, Vicki Ehlers. It was a copy of her book, *Green at Birth: How Smart Moms Make Nature Connections for Infants and Toddlers*. It was a real book written because of my program! I sat on my couch and read every word. I was a little bit stunned. My program actually worked! I was off and running, having one of my online virtual events every other month. In January 2009, I made $10,000, which every entrepreneur will tell you is a milestone — because if you can repeat it, you're on your way to six figures in a year. I was on a roll, though, and crossed six figures in June of that year.

What have been the key factors to your success and why?

Here are some of the things I did and now tell others to do.

First, take a chance. Good ideas live only in your mind until you commit to doing them and then take action. Take a chance and get them out there. Do more. Fail faster. Live your life, both business and personal, with no regrets!

Also, don't worry about what other people think. This is the best advice I received and remembered from my mother. Don't do things thinking about the reaction of others. Live for yourself first and foremost. (And the fact is people think about you far less than you think they do. They have their own problems going on.) And be okay with your decisions. Quit second guessing yourself. It's a path to hell on earth if you are constantly questioning the why of what you are doing. So first, make a decision, and then live it out!

On a related note, don't talk about your ideas with other people. I know loads of great book ideas that have never seen the 'page of day' because the aspiring author shared the idea with someone. It's not because that someone ran off to write the book themselves. Rather, they took out a pin and burst the aspiring author's bubble. It breaks my heart. Wayne Dyer said that dreams are like seeds you plant. You have to take extra special care of them during the beginning stages. Shelter sprouts from the harsh wind. Fertilize often. And then, when it's ready, show it to the world. Protect your dreams from others until they are strong enough to stand on their own.

Don't confuse lack of passion for "Should I do this at all?" I know Marsha Sinetar meant well when she directed people to "do what you love, and the money will follow," but really? I'll put it this way — I wasn't born with a passion for showing people how to write and publish a book. I started showing people because I had figured it out for myself. But then I started to get good at it. And then I started making money doing it. And then I developed a passion for it. As in I love it. I bounce out of bed every morning excited to talk to people about getting out of their own way and getting a book done. I now have a passion for it. But it didn't start out that way. It started out with a lot of work and even some doubt, but I plugged along. I made the decision to put the effort and the hours in every day, and then I fine-tuned my methods and messages along the way.

Remember to KISS (keep it super simple). I've a friend who can go from 'napkin idea' to empire in about two minutes flat. I love ideas, but even I have tripped myself up by making them too complicated at the start. Don't let the idea of 'great' hold you back from taking action on the idea of 'good'. Start small and build.

Savor the beginnings. You'll read below that I found my 'one thing' and the wheels started to move. I still love what I do, however part of me misses the excitement of starting something 'brand new' and putting it out there. The late nights at my computer, being kept company by the San Diego Padres baseball team, and the first dollars coming magically via email. Don't get me wrong, there are a lot of things to savor now that things are far less bumpy, but there is something special about beginnings. If that's where you're at, make sure you savor yours.

What do you do when you feel demotivated or overwhelmed?

Here are the mantras that keep me going as I continue on this journey of being an entrepreneur:

This too shall pass.

This one has been a life-long mantra after my parents died when I was 24. It comforts me in times of grief and also reminds me that even the good things shall pass. It's what we signed up for to be on this big, beautiful blue marble. So, enjoy the journey.

You've made it this far.

Whenever I have a 'panic moment' about something not working out, whether it's a new offering not getting sign-ups or wondering where the rest of the money will come from for the month, I think, "Well, I've made it this far." I've been on my own in San Diego for more than 15 years, so something has been working — and will continue to work.

Related to this, I think…

Question and understand.

If you talk to me for five minutes, you're likely to hear me ask you five questions. One of my specialties in understanding others is through questioning — not to interrogate, but to discover. If you want to connect with people on a deeper level fast, I recommend learning how to question in a way to understand where they are at and where they want to go.

Take the high road.

There's a little bit of danger in being a smart communicator. I can always prove my point 'debate style' or 'attorney style'. Although I've never been on a debate team and I'm not a lawyer, I have the tools to cut someone down and show I'm right. It's sometimes tempting to do so, especially when I get a bad review on my program or a nasty email from someone on my list. But then I tell myself to *take the high road*. It's not worth getting down on the low road with others — it takes me down with them. So, although I may think or even write the "You're wrong" response, I take the high road and don't send it.

Teach and the money will follow.

Secrets of Successful Authors and Publishers

Even if there's no official title, each of us is a teacher and a minister. You have a message to share, so go out there and share it whether it's through a book, speech or a blog. Don't keep your messages to yourself — get them out there. And when you do it consistently, with the right intention and follow-up, you can make a business and a success out of it!

You can learn more about Donna on her website
www.FreeBookPlanner.com

JYOTSNA RAMACHANDRAN:
Too Lazy to Write

I only met Jyotsna recently and we first connected over me inviting her to participate in this book. I found her fascinating and wanted you to meet her too.

Jyotsna relishes being a HomeEntrepreneur™ (stay-at-home mom + entrepreneur). Her journey towards freedom began when she decided never to be an employee ever again. She understood that in order to enjoy true freedom, she needed to create passive income streams. The best way to do that was to start online businesses. She now runs a book publishing company and coaches people on how they too can convert their passion into an online business.

When did you start considering yourself financially successful as an author? How long did it take after you published your first book? How did it feel and why?

I started publishing books even before I became an author! I was looking for ways to earn passive income online sometime in early 2014 when I came across this concept of self-publishing. Back then, I didn't have the confidence to write my own book, so I started to find profitable topics that were in trend and got the books written by ghostwriters. Within six months, I had published close to 50 books on various topics, ranging from health to business and from gardening to parenting. Slowly but steadily, my income from book royalties grew to $4,500 per month by January 2015. That gave me the confidence to write my first book called *Job Escape Plan,* which went on to become a No.1 bestseller in multiple categories, received more than 100 five-star reviews and was also listed in 2015 by Inc.com as one of the year's Top 10 books on business startup. It was a very fulfilling experience because it felt very good to know that so many people got inspired by reading my book and some of them even took action by starting their own businesses.

What have been the key factors to your success and why?

I can think of two factors which helped me reach where I am today.

One: determination

I was determined that I'd never be an employee ever again. It has been seven years since I quit my job and the very thought of going back to work in a corporate job scares me even today. Failing as an entrepreneur is, therefore, not an option. I have to make it work somehow.

Two: focus

I used to run four businesses simultaneously and none of them were giving me the desired results. Then I decided to shut all my other businesses and focus solely on publishing. Over the last three years, I'm doing just this one thing and that has given great results.

What has been your worst decision as a writer and how did you bounce back and still get to where you are today? Did this failure set you up for your current success?

One fine day, Amazon changed its rules and introduced this thing called KENP (where authors get paid for the number of pages read even if the reader doesn't buy the book). I didn't realize what a huge hit this could be. Before I could realize, my royalties dropped by 50 percent. Amazon ads was also a game changer. I was too late to join the AMS bandwagon and as a result lost a lot of money to competitors. Today, I keep my eyes and ears open to the changing trends and I also have a publishing service company, so Amazon is not my only source of income.

What has been your best decision as an author and why?

Helping other authors to get their books published by starting a service for them has been the best decision I've made as an author. I know my limitations as an author. I can't publish a book every two months like some of my successful author friends do, so I decided to use my resources (my team of writers, designers, editors, formatters, narrators, etc.) to serve other authors by starting a company called Happy Self Publishing years ago. We have so far worked with more than 300 authors from 25 countries.

What is the best investment you've made as an author and why?

The time, energy and money I've invested in content marketing in the form of videos, podcasts and blog posts has been the best investment I've made because most people discover me through my content. Then they start following me and eventually, they end up buying one of my products or services.

If you were deprived of all but one of your marketing tools, which would you keep and why?

Going as a guest on other people's podcasts has given me great results. And the best part is it doesn't cost any money! So, if I was deprived of all other marketing tools, I'd just go to iTunes and start reaching out to the hosts of podcasts that are relevant to my niche.

What is an unusual habit that you have as a writer that helps you succeed?

Although I love sharing my knowledge with the world, I'm too lazy to write. As I'm not passionate about writing, I was procrastinating about my second book for a long time. Finally, I found a method to solve this problem. I now record my ideas, concepts, insights etc. as an audio file and send it to a professional writer, who does a great job of converting my voice into a book. I now offer this service called Angel Writing to my clients as well as it's a boon for aspiring authors who don't have the time or skill to write. We guide them from rough idea to helping them select a book topic, outline their concepts into a structured table of contents and then interview them for 5-6 hours over a period of two weeks to get all the information we need to write the chapters. Once the authors approve the rough draft, we go ahead and elaborate and write the final draft.

What would you have done differently if you were to start your writing career with the knowledge you have now?

I would've definitely written and published more books in a consistent manner. I would've also engaged more with my readers through emails and by building a community for them on Facebook. When I wrote my first book, I didn't have a business behind the book (like an online course or coaching program). My second book called *Book Your Success*, which I'm writing now, is totally aligned with my publishing service business. I now look at a book as just the first level of engagement with my audience. We can serve them at a much higher level by offering coaching/consulting services, having an online course, sharing affiliate products, creating a done-for-you service or even conducting live workshops.

What bad advice do you often hear on the subject of self-publishing and book-marketing?

One thing I hear from many self-published authors is that they have to do everything themselves. This is the perfect recipe for disaster. Most authors do not take the professional help of designers and try to use Canva templates to design their cover. Canva is an amazing software which even I use for many things, but definitely not for designing my book cover myself. Another costly mistake could be asking your friend or cousin to edit your book to save some money. Unless that person is a professional editor who has the experience of editing books, I'd discourage you from doing that. Self-publishing doesn't mean you should do everything yourself. Authors should outsource parts of the publishing process to people who are experts at it. This drastically improves the quality of the book and saves a ton of time for the author which can be used for marketing the book. Who says that a self-published book cannot look like a *New York Times* bestseller?

What do you do when you feel demotivated or overwhelmed?

Yes, there are days when I lack motivation or feel overwhelmed. On those days, I try to reconnect with my purpose of why I'm doing what I'm doing. I started with self-publishing so that I could work from home to be around my children and also make a good profit to enjoy a great lifestyle with my family. When I relook at my vision board, it automatically motivates me to focus on my work. When the tasks at hand overwhelm me, my journal comes to my rescue. I list out the activities based on priority and classify them into what should be done by me now, what can be done by me later and what can be delegated to my team. This lets me maintain my sanity!

What's your advice for authors who are still struggling?

If you are not making the amount of money that you want to from your books, it could be due to four reasons.

The topic

You've chosen a very narrow niche and there is hardly anyone who is interested in it. Go to Amazon to check how the other books in that topic are doing. If none of them are selling well, it may be an indication that the readership for that topic is too small. Look at writing your next book on a broader topic. It would be a good idea to choose a broader, more popular niche and then write multiple books that each go deep into covering one main idea.

The content

Your book's quality may not be good enough. If your book is in a category where other books are doing well, then it's time to check if your book's content is valuable enough. Read the negative reviews you've been getting. That should give you an idea about what to improve. If it's a fiction book, you may want to make it more engaging. If it's a nonfiction book, try to make it more actionable and practical with loads of useful resources.

The packaging

You've not packaged the book well to convince the reader to hit the buy button. So see if you can improve the book's title, subtitle or cover to make it more attractive. Check if the book's description can be written using powerful copywriting language that'll persuade the reader to buy the book. You may also want to change the book's categories and keywords to improve the searchability on Amazon.

The marketing

You've not been marketing the book well. If you've taken care of the above three points and your book is still not selling well, then it's time you put efforts into marketing the book. Collaborate with other people in your niche to add value to their audience (and also market your book to them).

Run price-discount promotions every once in a while, book yourself as a speaker in industry forums, take advantage of Amazon ads, Facebook ads etc. Have a marketing plan and allocate a budget to keep promoting your book.

Most successful authors take care of these four things and then focus on writing a catalogue of books under that category. This is the time-tested approach which every full-time author uses.

If you've not yet published your books, you can check out Jyotsna's free seven-day book kickstart challenge at www.happyselfpublishing.com/challenge.

You can also reach out to her at

jyotsna@happyselfpublishing.com.

RISTEN JOY LAIDIG: I Feel What I Want to Do Before I Do It

The first time I connected with Kristen was when I invited her to be part of this book. Co-operation is a wonderful thing and co-authoring a book is a great excuse to make friends!

Kristen decided she was 'unemployable' at the tender age of 6 when she started her first business making and selling pet rocks with nothing but a Sharpie® marker, gravel and a little creativity. A serial entrepreneur, in 2003, she turned her lifelong love of writing into a full-time career teaching authors and entrepreneurs how to create books that bring them business and turning authors into successful authorpreneurs through her internationally-known brand, The Book Ninja®.

She currently changes lives through her students one published message at a time, invests in start-up companies, manages her own book and toy store (*Toy Box Gifts &Wonder*) in the heart of her newfound hometown, Chambersburg, PA, is in the startup phase of at least three new businesses at any given time, and consults existing business owners who are ready to level up their game.

When did you start considering yourself financially successful as an author? How long did it take after you published your first book? How did it feel and why?

Since I first entered the world of publishing as marketing director for a startup self-publisher in 2003, I've gone on to publish more than 35 books of my own and more than 200 books written by others. The first book I ever 'wrote' was a journal for children to keep track of their friends' odd interests. It was a test to make sure we knew what we were doing with the company workflow, so I honestly never expected it to be much of a success. I was surprised when it started selling hundreds of copies each summer with no marketing. I'd simply put it out there as a sample of what our company could do and I focused on marketing the company's publishing services. Those royalties were an unexpected joy and encouraged me to keep creating more books.

In 2013, I put myself on the publishing map by doing what I at first thought was an impossible challenge from my coach — publishing 18 Kindle books in 18 weeks. Each book averaged around 10,000 words and was completely written, edited, designed and formatted for Kindle within seven days. It was exhausting! I think I averaged around four hours of sleep each night and I know my sanity only survived due to my high chocolate consumption. And yet I learned an invaluable lesson through that whole experience. If you want to capture the attention of a market, do something extraordinary within that market.

While I'd never do it again, I can attribute the turning point of my entire business to that *one* event. That self-challenge launched my bestselling Kindle in 30 Challenge, which shifted my career from done-for-you publishing services in which I could only service up to 15 people per year to online training for authors, which enabled me to reach tens of thousands of people per year. By doing that one little extraordinary act, my monthly income tripled, I was able to increase the size of my staff, and I discovered I had a knack for (and more importantly, a taste for) training.

What have been the key factors to your success and why?

Because I started in the business of publishing and business has always had my heart, I've often been a little further ahead than most 'starving authors'. I've always seen books as a marketing tool for my business, rather than books being my sole business. And therein I believe lies the secret to true authorpreneurial success: the ability to build a business with your books. That's why I do everything I do from a position of marketing.

The title, subtitle, branding, content, website, social media pages, etc. are all created with the question "How will this sell more books?" in mind. With my latest book, *Asskickonomics: the powerful unseen force behind every entrepreneur*, I mentioned several of my products as examples, named my retail stores, and carefully crafted my words to make soft recommendations of the accompanying workbook and journal. I believe my ability to integrate marketing into every single section of a project is one of the foundational keys to my success.

Success isn't without failure. I love how people seem to think I became an overnight success. The truth is I'm a 12-years-in-the-making success. I've hired the wrong team members, had to fire assistants, VAs and employees, and contributed to a lot of my own stress by worrying about things like cash flow.

My husband and I now have two retail stores and eight employees, which amounts to about $15,000 in payroll each month. This cost doesn't include our regular business expenses and VAs for our online businesses that currently *fund* those stores. If I had to say I had one failure that was bigger than all the rest, I'd say my hiring process was too trusting.

While I firmly believe it's nearly impossible to make more than $500,000 per year without having outside help, I've also learned to be much more strategic during the hiring process. I'm usually slow to fire, and sometimes that brings me additional grief. But I also believe in giving humans a chance. However, there comes a point in time when you have to say "enough is enough" and look for help elsewhere. Now we have processes and systems in place to ensure employees do what is expected of them, and I've incorporated much of that into my online business as well.

What has been your best decision as an author (writing and/or marketing) and why?

To that end, the best decision I ever made was to start outsourcing. I know I just complained about hiring the wrong people. But the fact is outsourcing is what's made my business grow. I started with hiring a housekeeper and accountant. The month I hired my first housekeeper my business income tripled. The next month, I hired my accountant and that new number doubled again. It seemed every time I outsourced something I hated to do to someone who thrived on doing that task, my income grew.

I was able to focus more than just time, but something much more valuable on growing my business — *brainspace*. I'm always thinking about business... how I can sell more books, what new trainings I can create, how I can get people into our stores... business. I seem to live and breathe marketing, and if it weren't for my decision to start outsourcing the tasks I didn't enjoy, I wouldn't be able to run five different companies and countless programs and events today.

If you were deprived of all but one of your marketing tools, which would you keep and why?

I've talked a lot about marketing and that's really a huge key to success. I've a friend who preaches, "Your fortune is in your follow-up." While I'm quite certain she didn't originate that phrase, it's true. Follow-up takes many forms. Some people think it's an autoresponder sequence. Others think it's calling people you chat with on social media. Still others think it's cold-calling people whose business cards you randomly picked up at that last writer's event.

Follow-up is simply staying in touch. And due to my love of writing and my favorite marketing platform being social media, the one tool I'd always save in order to activate this powerful form of marketing is Facebook. It makes follow-up (staying in touch) easy!

What is an unusual habit that you have as a writer that helps you succeed?

It's been proven time and again that successful people all share one quality — the importance they place on creating good habits. Those habits may range from writing morning pages to spending 15 seconds in a cryogenic chamber freezing your you-know-what off. I've studied a lot of successful people and they sure can have some quirky habits!

My own habits stray away from the rigidness of many successful entrepreneurs that say you must have a strict schedule, you must do XYZ every morning, you must limit your time on social media to 10 minutes per day and so on and so forth. I prefer to go with my gut. I've developed a habit of *feeling*. I *feel* what I want to do before I do it. I get inspired to create a new project or write a new book and I jump on it. If I'm not inspired or *feel* it, I don't force it. Instead, I find something I do feel like doing and focus on that.

When I was writing *Asskickonomics* (which took about two years from idea to completion), I only worked on it when I *felt* like working on it. I didn't force a certain number of words per day. I didn't make myself sit down and write. Instead, I went with my gut. Any time I started to get overwhelmed, I'd make a to-do list of everything I needed to get done that day and put a * next to the one that *had* to get done *that day*. Then, after I completed the one with the * next to it, I'd look at my list again and ask myself, "What do I *feel* like doing?"

Sometimes what I felt like doing wasn't on my list at all. And instead of feeling guilty and 'shoulding' (more on that in my book) all over myself for failing my to-dos, I focused on what I *felt* like doing. What I discovered was that by satisfying my emotionally-charged ideas and working on those first, it actually gave me even *more* energy to apply to the to-dos that I'd rather put off. And that included getting my book written.

What would you have done differently if you were to start your writing career with the knowledge you have now?

While I'd love to make decisions to avoid the pain I've endured through lost money, screwed-up projects, bad relationships, etc., the fact is if I hadn't made those decisions I wouldn't be who I am today.

Success isn't necessarily how much money you have in the bank, although that can be a huge part of it. It's more about *who* you have become. Have you allowed your struggles to define who you are and your ability to be successful? Or have you become a success *in spite of* those struggles? Nobody is unique in struggle. Everyone has issues. Everyone has loss. Everyone experiences pain. It's called being human. What makes you different is how you choose to handle the negative side of life. You may have had your dream of being an author abused, in that people told you it wasn't worth it or you shouldn't pursue it. After all, it's only one tiny step up from being a 'starving artist'.

What bad advice do you often hear on the subject of self-publishing and book-marketing?

The number one thing so-called gurus teach is "Follow the money". They tell you to search those keywords on Amazon. Look at what's bestselling in a category. Look at what *categories* are bestselling… then write for *that* market. No mention of what you might *want* to write. No mention of how you *feel* about said category.

Nothing enrages me more than people that tell you your dream is worthless and that you shouldn't follow your passion because there's no money in it. I've seen artists charge more than $5,000 for one painting... and get it. I've seen authors write their passion and then sell *millions* of books.

The biggest mistake you could ever make is to follow the advice of those 'gurus' and write purely for the market. *You* are the best salesperson for your book and message. Are you really willing to commit to promote something you hated creating simply because it has your name on it? I highly doubt you'd waste your time marketing something you hated creating, just because the category was 'proven' to sell.

Motivation comes in many forms and money is simply one of them. Most authors and artists I've met are motivated by much more than simply money alone.

What do you do when you feel demotivated or overwhelmed?

Feeling demotivated typically accompanies a sense of being overwhelmed. You may have become overwhelmed researching your publishing options or reading conflicting reports of the best printers.

I've discovered that authors and entrepreneurs typically overwhelm themselves by looking ahead and trying to figure out their future steps before they're remotely ready for them. And when that happens, they often shut down, lose their passion and drive, and stop *feeling* the desire to complete their projects.

When I get overwhelmed I physically take a step back. I get out of my office chair, *feel* where I'm at right now, then take an actual real-life step back. I even move my legs to do it. Then I take a deep breath and look at my project in my mind's eye and ask this all-important question:

"What is the very, very, very next thing, not the 10th thing, not the 3rd thing, but the very next tiny thing that I need to do next?"

I break down whatever it is I need to do to a *tiny* next step. Then, with a deep breath, I realize I *can* do this. The energy flows back, the passion sparks again, and I *feel* ready.

What's your advice for authors who are still struggling?

The cycle of becoming overwhelmed happens to all of us. It can be triggered by the weather, a bad day, getting in over your head, promising something you can't deliver, tech going wrong, research that leads to more questions than answers, etc. And if you're not careful, that cycle can become a *normal* state of life; what I call your 'normalcy trap' in *Asskickonomics*.

A normalcy trap is the most dangerous place you can permanently reside, and it's *the source* of your struggles because it only exists if you're getting something out of it. Your normalcy traps can be easily identified in areas where you struggle. Do you often find your bank account dipping well below what's comfortable, then suddenly push yourself to create something new and the cash flows in? Then you may have a normalcy trap of 'saving the day' or playing the hero in your business. Do you 'should' on yourself a lot or put yourself down? Then you have a normalcy trap that makes others pity you or come to your rescue. I live with both these traps and they're incredibly common!

The good news is you can break out of *any* normalcy trap. All you have to do is become aware of its existence and put steps into place to get out of it next time you find yourself sliding in. Those steps begin with finding accountability with a mentor, coach or friend, who has permission to point out when you're sneaking or diving head first into your normalcy traps and to help pull you out when you find yourself deeply entrenched in one.

Connect with Kristen on a personal level at www.KristenJoysBlog.com. You can get your free Book Publishing Checklist at www.thebookninja.com.

PART 5: TRAINERS

ALEXA BIGWARFE: Ditch the Negative Nancies

When I met Alexa, we hit it off immediately. She invited me to run one of my webinars to her audience and to speak at the ALLI Self-Publishing Conference.

Alexa is a mother, author, publisher, entrepreneur and podcaster. Her writing career began after her infant daughter died at 2 days old. She has written and/or edited and self-published numerous books of her own and for other authors through her hybrid publishing company, Kat Biggie Press. She uses that hard-earned publishing knowledge to support other writers and small businesses in completing, publishing and marketing their books through her company Write.Publish.Sell. Her podcast of the same name has recently launched, featuring authors and publishing topics.

When did you start considering yourself financially successful as an author? How long did it take after you published your first book? How did it feel and why?

If you decided to write a book to make a lot of money, be prepared for a lot of ups and downs. The most important thing for authors to understand is there are many ways of doing it. You need to determine what works best for you. Don't just try to replicate what worked for someone else.

Some authors make most of their money from book sales. But for many of us (particularly nonfiction writers, which is my area of expertise), our largest revenue sources come from the by-product of our writing. I'm not one of the authors that you'll see promoting how to sell 1 million copies of a book because my success has largely been the result of outside-of-the-box thinking, promotion and partnerships, and author support services. Results can't be tracked by looking only at book sales and rankings. I didn't get there quickly but I stayed consistent, and within two years of publishing my first book, I was making a full-time income through book sales and author support services.

It's important to understand that I didn't publish my first book to make any money at all. My husband and I had suffered a tremendous loss. Our 2-day-old infant died and her surviving twin spent 84 days in the Neonatal Intensive Care Unit. I began blogging as an outlet for my grief and a way to raise awareness on infant and maternal health. After almost two years, I decided to write a book so that grieving parents would have a resource to help guide them through life after loss. My first book, *Sunshine After the Storm: A Survival Guide for the Grieving Mother*, which includes advice and stories from 30 other grieving parents, was not written to be a bestseller or to make a lot of money. My intent in writing the book was to provide it to families, hospitals and bereavement groups free of charge. Yes, *free*. I also offer it to support organizations at just barely above wholesale cost. Sometimes money isn't the reason we write books.

I didn't enter the writing and publishing world looking for fame or fortune. But I *did* fall in love with writing and publishing books. I wanted to do more, so I started writing about parenting and motherhood. To be honest, I had no idea how to market books when we launched *Lose the Cape: realities for busy modern moms and strategies to survive*. It didn't have a massive launch either, and I struggled with feeling like a real loser. I wasn't a loser. I just didn't know what I was doing. Many first-time authors find themselves in the same place. Learn from it and get better! I realized a few important things with the second book. Firstly, if you don't have a platform or audience, you won't sell many books. Secondly, it doesn't matter how great the book is if no one finds it when they're searching Amazon.

From this point, I began to invest heavily in learning all things related to publishing and marketing a good book. I wanted to create high-quality books and I wanted to help other women like me who had an important story to share. As more people started approaching me to help them publish their books, I realized I had an author support business in the making. Three years into my writing career, when I signed my first big contract to produce, publish and market a book for someone else, I knew I was going to be able to make a living from my writing and publishing. The more I do this for other people, the better I make my own books. I'm learning new techniques and tactics with every launch and I'm retroactively applying those to my own books. My first book was published almost five years ago, and it continues to have steady sales, with little effort on my part. And that feels glorious.

What have been the key factors to your success and why?

There is no one *right* way. But there are a few things you can do to help yourself. I credit my success to this factor: you *must* start with your *why* and you have to know and understand your goal in publishing. Why is the *why* and the goal so important? There are so many different strategies to help you achieve success. If you try to implement a hodge-podge mixture, or just emulate what someone else did, you're going to spin your wheels non-stop and get frustrated. You may not see results. If, however, you understand why you're writing a book and what you hope to achieve with that book, you will have a better chance of creating a marketing plan and implementing a strategy that will help you achieve your goal.

For example, my *why* was to publish a book that helped parents who were grieving the loss of a pregnancy or a child. My goal was to get the book into as many hands as needed it, at no cost. My marketing strategy consisted of activities that would help achieve my goals and my *why* kept me on track. I began to blog frequently on grief and infant loss; words to say to someone who lost a baby; and how to help a family after their loss. I made sure my SEO was top notch and I created cornerstone content that continues to drive people to my website. I made sure my book was suggested on each of those pages. 90 percent of my book sales continue to come through my website.

My goal didn't include bestseller status or high levels of income from the book for grieving mothers. So I approached organizations that send care packages to grieving parents as well as organizations that serve this group, and I provide the book to them as a donation or at very low cost. I use the money that comes from sales to pay for more donated books.

If my *why* had been to create a source of income and my goal had been to make as much money as possible from book sales, I'd have taken a completely different approach and laid out a strategy that was representative of those two factors. So spend some time thinking about your *why* and your goals and then research the best marketing tactics to make those things happen. Develop a plan and implement it. Remember that for most of us, it's a marathon, not a sprint. And never forget you have to know who your target audience is and how you can get in front of them.

What has been your worst decision as an author and how did you bounce back and still get to where you are today? Did this failure set you up for your current success?

It happens to all of us! This whole adventure is constant trial and error. Figure out what works and do more of that and scratch the activities that are sucking your money out and not producing results. I've made plenty of bad decisions along this journey and spent a lot of money that I wish I'd spent more wisely. My biggest mistake was trying to be too broad in my strategy and failing because I tried to do too much. When I first started trying to market *Lose the Cape,* my second book (the first book I wanted to go big with), I tried to do too much. I was going to use Facebook ads, set up a book funnel and get that book everywhere. I wasted a lot of time and energy and money buying courses on how to do all of those things. Instead, I should have been concentrating on growing my audience, building relationships and growing my email list so that I had people to sell the book to and an audience to target with my ads and efforts. I wish I could have that time and money back. That's not to say that those marketing streams are not a good thing. They can be used and implemented to result in amazing success. But I tried to do it all at once, I tried to do it all myself instead of just hiring people who do this for a living and know what they are doing, and I failed. Miserably. Now, I rely on others to help me with the systems and tools I don't have a clue about. I focus my efforts more on gaining visibility and building my audience and network. I've realized that a focused strategy is far more effective than a blanket approach. And I know that a solid email list and a big audience network (of your real fans, not fake fans) is the best way to sell books, programs, courses and more. And a free tip — I've found that press releases generally are a big waste of money.

What has been your best decision as an author and why?

I started seeing a lot more success when I decided to hire a team. Bringing on a virtual assistant and finding other freelancers that I have created ongoing relationships with — like social media managers, graphic artists and Facebook Ads managers that I can turn to when I'm ramping up for a launch or other promotions — has allowed me to focus more on the big picture, the writing, the strategy, the platform development and allows me to put the other elements that are not in my wheelhouse or area of expertise in the hands of people who do them well. Yes, it can be expensive to hire them but I assure you, I wasted more on poor-performing ads than it cost to hire someone who did Facebook ads with great success for me. Sometimes it's just worth it to let other people do what they are good at. My virtual assistant helps me across the board with pitching for more visibility for podcasts and blogs, managing my calendar and running the author support business I have created.

My best investments have been along these same lines: investing in expertise and help but also in professional development and service organizations that are dedicated to helping me learn and grow as an author and publisher. I've spent a lot of time and money honing my skills, learning the crafts of publishing and marketing, and becoming an expert at what I do. Unfortunately, my own writing and marketing efforts fell by the wayside as I learned how to do this best for others. I've recently returned to writing and publishing my own books and the investment in my education is really paying off!

If I had to pick one thing, though, my best investment has been in relationship building, networking and collaborative efforts. I've learned so much by working with others, interviewing others, participating in conferences and summits, and projects like this one. We say it takes a village to raise a family but I'd also say it takes a village to raise a successful author.

If you were deprived of all your marketing tools and could keep only one, which would it be and why?

The one I'd keep over all others is my blog. This probably surprises you but I've seen over the years what well-written content and content that is backed by a solid search-engine optimization strategy can do for book sales, audience growth and the best sales tool — your email list. I love to help authors realize how they can use their blog to draw in an audience that they can't necessarily reach through social media and other efforts. There are so many amazing marketing tools available, both paid and unpaid, but at the end of the day, your efforts should be geared largely toward the places and spaces that you own — your website, your blog and your email list. If you've done the work you need to do in these areas, everything else flows much more easily.

What is an unusual habit that you have as an author that helps you succeed?

I don't know if this constitutes a habit or a quirk but I'm an over-sharer. I love to share my life experiences with others and I love to hear others. So, maybe that success habit really is listening because I learn so much from the experiences of others and their life lessons. And these play out in my blogging, my fiction (still unpublished but coming soon!) and my nonfiction books. I also think that this desire to learn about others and their stories makes me a phenomenal author coach and publisher.

What would you have done differently if you were to start your career with the knowledge you have now?

I'd start focusing on building my author platform, my email list and relationships far, far earlier. I was so busy trying to learn how to code my website, set up funnels and create the perfect audience for Facebook ads that I didn't spend time doing the things I should have been doing — creating content, writing and developing an audience to sell it to *before*

I was trying to sell the books. You can't make up lost time in those areas, but you can start right now! Create a landing page with a good lead magnet and start building that list (if you aren't already doing so!)

What bad advice do you often hear on the subject of online business and authorship?

"Don't spend money on publishing" — that is the stupidest thing I've ever seen people write in groups and forums, and I see it a lot. Yes, you do need to be aware — there are a lot of predatory agencies and businesses that are in the business of taking money from authors. So, yes, you need to do your due diligence when looking at paying for services and even hybrid publishing, which is a partner model in which the author assumes some of the financial burden of preparing the book for publishing in exchange for much higher royalties (starting at 50 percent or more). But to tell someone they shouldn't pay for services to get their book published because they can do it all on their own… it's just not a good idea. There are very few of us who are gifted graphic artists, writers, marketers, data miners, etc., especially straight out of the gate. These are skills you should hire out and/or take time to learn. There is so much to learn about publishing and marketing a high-quality book, and there is absolutely nothing wrong with hiring experts to help you through any of the elements of production, publication and marketing.

What do you do when you feel demotivated or overwhelmed?

I take a break from my work. I go for a walk. I connect with friends. I watch a funny show. I listen to podcasts. But I get away from it.

Affirmations are great too. Creatives fear failure, so if you can find ways to pump yourself up, that's awesome. Look at what *is* going well and ruminate on that for a while! Exercise is one of the best ways to get those creative juices flowing.

What's your advice for entrepreneurs who are still struggling?

I get it. I've watched many, many authors struggle with writing, publishing and selling their books. It's hard work. I relate it to parenting. No one ever told me how hard it would be. I just saw pictures of adorable newborns, hilarious toddlers and adoring school-aged children, and thought that's what it was all about. Wrong. There are many wonderful elements of being an authorpreneur, but there's a lot of work to be done too.

I recommend two things. Accountability groups (paid or free, although people tend to do more of the work and actually get it done when they pay for something!) or hiring a coach, publishing partner, book shepherd, hybrid publisher or someone like that. Find other people that you can relate to that can help you push through. And ditch the negative Nancies in your life. They just hold you back. A healthy writer mindset is hugely important to our success as creative indies. Register here: http://bit.ly/writermindset

> Alexa would love to help you in any way that she can. She offers a wide variety of free and paid services. A great place to start is her free Author Support Group on Facebook called Write.Publish.Sell (www.facebook.com/groups/WritePublishSell/). Her website offers free resources and links to each of her courses and training programs. www.writepublishsell.co. Or you can email her at info@writepublishsell.co

DANIEL HALL: Strive for Excellence, Not Perfection

I connected with Daniel only recently but we hit it off immediately. I interviewed him for the 5-Figure Author Challenge and shared his training on Pinterest for authors with my audience.

Daniel is an author, speaker, consultant, coach and host of the iTunes top-rated podcast Real Fast Results. He's also the creator of the popular Real Fast training programs designed to help authors, speakers, coaches, consultants, trainers, Internet marketers and entrepreneurs effectively grow their businesses faster and profit more effortlessly.

When did you start considering yourself financially successful as an author? How long did it take after publishing your first book? How did it feel, and why?

As a young, freshly-minted lawyer, I discovered a way to trade my speaking talents for free cruises for me and a traveling companion. Whenever I could break away from my law practice, I would travel the world in luxury as an 'enrichment' speaker for Royal Caribbean and Celebrity Cruises. As it turns out, this was a coveted speaking opportunity, and friends and colleagues began to seek me out so that they too could get free cruises using this pathway. I began privately teaching people how it was done but soon discovered that the demand was too great for me to teach one on one.

I decided to sit down and write out an eight-point checklist of how to trade speaking services for free luxury cruises. When I started the process, I thought my checklist would be a five-page 'special report' that I intended on selling to all the people who kept asking me for help. But what started out as a short checklist ended up becoming an exhaustive 130-page manuscript. I had my manuscript professionally edited and I published it as an ebook called *Speak on Cruise Ships: 8 easy steps to a lifetime of free luxury cruises*.

I figured out how to put up a simple sales page with an 'add to cart' button so I could collect money. By the way, I was able to do this even though I was not a coder or web designer because I taught myself basic HTML with free training through www.w3schools.com, which is run by the same folks who determine the HTML conventions.

Looking back, it's hilarious how bad this site looked (if you're interested check out SpeakersCruiseFree.com on the Wayback Machine at www.archive.org/web). Yet, regardless of its lack of design aesthetic, the website and the ebook it sold were instantly successful.

Within an hour of the website going live, I had my first order. I watched as another and then another came in, all without me promoting it. Apparently, Google had picked up my site and started showing it in the search results of anyone searching for "public speaking".

Not only was my ebook selling for $37 a copy but because the book was digitally delivered, that $37 price represented almost pure profit. I was hooked! Eventually, I raised the price of my ebook to $97. Instead of hurting sales, as I feared it would, sales actually improved. That ebook has gone on to generate more than a quarter of a million dollars in revenue and continues to sell to this day on Amazon.

In this process, I learned a fair amount about indie publishing and book marketing. I've gone on to do many more books, membership sites, audiobooks and courses. In doing so, I've generated literally millions of dollars in revenue. But here's the thing: it all came from my ability to write and my willingness to try something new.

As I reflect on my journey so far, there are a number of lessons that I believe could help you.

1. As Joseph Campbell, author of *The Hero with a Thousand Faces*, advised, "Follow your bliss." There are many ways to interpret this statement but the way I do it is that you should be open to and have a willingness to follow your inner nudges and inspirations. I know I've done very well as an author and publisher by being open-minded and unafraid of failure. There is a corollary to this lesson, however, and that is to fail fast and fail forward. I've had far more failures than I've had successes. Yes, failures can hurt, but I've found that persistence and a willingness to pivot almost always wins the day. Applied to your writing, this means you should be fearless in pursuing your ideas on the one hand but also be willing to adapt whatever it is you're putting out to market conditions

as you develop data from market research. If I have one regret, it's that I often wait too long to act. I tend to analyze and second guess way too often. Author, friend and star of The Secret, Joe Vitale, has said that "money loves speed". Effectively, this means don't wait to act. If money loves speed, you should too!

2. Often things don't go exactly as planned. This is difficult but there's almost always something positive that comes from your attempts. Doors tend to open and new opportunities appear by just putting yourself out there. Embrace that fact. Think of yourself as a surfer riding the waves of opportunity that come your way. You're never quite sure how far (or even if) a wave will take you but you will float aimlessly without trying.

3. Assume that people want your content in multiple formats. When I wrote *Speak on Cruise Ships*, if I had been set on waiting until I could find a traditional publisher, I would still be waiting. The market was too small for such a highly niche book. Regardless, I put it out for very little money as an ebook and it has made me a small fortune. One side note here is that as my book was so highly niche, I was able to get away with selling it for $97. Consider how rare and desirable your content is when you price it and don't be in a hurry to charge less than or equal to what other books cost. I've found that people will respect your content more if you're charging more money for it. On the other hand, if you start high and the content is not selling, don't be afraid to lower the price. Once again, ride the wave that is the market and adjust as you go. If you have a book or writing project that you've been wanting to do, consider independently publishing that content in a more accessible format. For

example, I use Amazon's print-on-demand service at www.createspace.com/ to publish physical books. I also use the Ingram print-on-demand service www.ingramspark.com/ to make my books available to libraries and retailers. Amazon's Audiobook Creation Exchange at www.acx.com/ publishes my books as audiobooks. Author's Republic at www.authorsrepublic.com/ publishes my audiobooks to all other online retailers and also makes them available to libraries for licensing. Kindle Direct Publishing at www.kdp.amazon.com helps to publish my ebooks. Finally, I use Draft 2 Digital at www.draft2digital.com/ to publish my ebooks on every other online retailer. The point is that as an indie author, you can get to the same marketplaces that the marquee authors published by the New York trade publishers can. You can go toe to toe with them, and if your work is good and resonates with the marketplace, it's even possible to outsell them. That's what I love; agents and big publishing houses don't decide whether your work is worthy — the marketplace decides, and they vote with their dollars.

4. Do your best work but don't fawn over it for so long that you never put it out. My good friend Rita Emmett, author of *The Procrastinator's Handbook*, says you should strive for excellence, not perfection. Granted this is a balancing act but learn when good enough is good enough and get on to marketing or the next project.

5. This is probably the most important lesson I can teach: build your platform as you go. When I say platform, I'm talking about building a group of fans of you and your work. It's never too early to start either. The best way to build this platform is by collecting names and email addresses. You do this by offering something free and valuable that your target

demographic will find appealing. Often you can make this offer within the pages of your book as well as on your author website or blogs. Essentially, you trade your free goodie for their name and email address. Yes, you will need an email service provider. I recommend the free plan offered by Benchmark (www.danielhallpresents.com/benchmark); it will allow you to collect and mail your first 2,000 subscribers for free.

Daniel invites you to check out some free content — it's a video tutorial called "How to Publish Your Blog to Amazon's Kindle Platform to Create a Micro-Membership Site!". It's embedded on this page right now — www.danielhallpresents.com/getcode. There are eight other writing/publishing tutorials that you get if you opt in to his community.

LISE CARTWRIGHT: Done is Better than Perfect

I met Lise a few years ago and interviewed her for my 5-Figure Author Challenge. I also invited her as a guest lecturer to speak at my Author Remake mastermind. She's full of energy and Kiwi enthusiasm!

Lise has no special degrees in writing, nor has she sought any awards. Lise writes because she loves to share her knowledge with the world, inspiring hope and a way forward for authors to do what they love, one person at a time. Lise resides in beautiful New Zealand with her Australian hubby. She writes nonfiction books about health and wellness, entrepreneurship and writing, while helping authors navigate the business side of running a successful author business.

When did you start considering yourself financially successful as an author? How long did it take after you published your first book? How did it feel and why?

When I decided that I wanted to become an author, it was because I wanted to add another income stream to my freelance writing business. Little did I know that within a few short months, I'd be getting rid of all of my freelance clients and going full-time as an author.

I consider any venture successful when I hit $1,000 per month. For my first book, that took about four months to achieve. I wrote my first book in 2014 and published it that September. I had no idea what was going to happen next. I'll never forget getting the first KDP notification from Amazon in my inbox. It came in around the 23rd of the month and all it said was:

"KDP Royalty Notification — Lise Cartwright

This royalty payment notification is for Kindle Direct Publishing (KDP) sales recorded in the US Kindle Store. Payment will be made to your bank account and should appear in your available balance within two to five business days after the Payment Date. Details of the payment will be available on the Payment Report (www.kdp.amazon.com/self-publishing/reports) after it has been processed by your bank. If your KDP account is registered on the KDP Japan site, you can check your Payment Report at www.kdp.amazon.co.jp/self-publishing/reports."

To see the amount, I had to log into my KDP dashboard. I remember doing just that and not believing my eyes when, right in front of me on the screen, was a dollar sign followed by four digits. It felt amazing; freeing; like I could do this and make a full-time living from it. It was at this point that I knew I was financially successful as an author and that if I could do that with one book, I could do it with more.

What have been the key factors to your success and why?

1. Consistently publishing

I realized early on that to be successful as an author, I had to treat my writing like a business. This meant a regular publishing schedule, much like you would with a podcast or physical product.

If I was going to make money doing this, I needed to be regularly releasing new books to my hungry readers.

2. Production schedule

Once I decided I was going to need to publish frequently, I pulled out my calendar and worked out what that would be like in reality. It meant working out how many books I could write in a year (10-12 has been my average for a while), what types of launches I was going to do and all the other things involved in maintaining a book business. Without this schedule, none of my books would get written.

3. Systems

To produce this amount of content, I knew that I was going to need to have my own systems in place. I didn't want to drop the ball on my coaching business or leave myself so busy that things would start to unravel (which they did in the beginning!). It's about using tools like Trello (to keep track of each book project), writing inside Scrivener, having an editor that edits inside Scrivener and working with a cover designer who understands my brand. I know the process inside out for producing a book, and I follow it every time. If I deviate from the plan, things start to fall apart. Systems make it easy to maintain my publishing schedule.

4. Being plugged in

Being around other authors has been key for my success. I'm fairly isolated out here in New Zealand, so being able to connect with other authors online is a lifesaver. If I'm struggling or Amazon's done something weird, I know I can reach out to a few people and get help right away. Having that network, that community, is the main reason I continue to do what I do, because I have their support. There's nothing quite like having your own cheer squad to lift you up when you're feeling down!

What has been your worst decision as a writer and how did you bounce back and still get to where you are today? Did this failure set you up for your current success?

At the beginning of 2016, I started seeing more and more people creating courses. It was a case of 'shiny object syndrome' and I completely followed Alice and went down the rabbit hole. I wasted more than 12 months focusing on building courses instead of writing books and it cost me dearly. I didn't have a big enough email list to sustain the launch side of things needed for courses and I was well out of my depth.

By the beginning of 2017, I felt lost, disillusioned with my entire business and ready to give up. Thankfully, my husband said to me one night, "Why don't you go back to writing books? You were so happy when you were doing that." So while I figured out what writing books looked like again for me, I also pivoted and started coaching and consulting with other authors. This was the inspiration that I needed to get back to writing books and things have only improved since then.

Getting side tracked and then coming back full circle set me up for my current success. I'm able to tell my coaching clients *not* to create a course until they have a large enough audience to sustain a launch. Everything happens for a reason, and now I have more to share from a knowledge perspective, which means... more books to write!

What has been your best decision as an author (writing and/or marketing) and why?

That's deciding to publish regularly. I'm so lucky that I can do this full-time and even luckier that I get to do something that I love. Deciding to become a full-time author has been one of the best decisions I've made in my life. Without it, I would not be where I am today. Writing is such a joy for me — and being able to impact others makes my heart sing.

I know it sounds a little woo-woo, but I enjoy helping others. The goal of every single book I write is to change the life of just one person. If the book does that, then I consider it a success.

What is the best investment you've made as an author and why? (could be an investment of money, time or energy)

Back in 2014, a few months after our wedding, I remember catching the tail end of a webinar with Chandler Bolt and his old business partner James. They were laughing, having a ton of fun and dropping some massive knowledge bombs with regard to writing and publishing a book. Up until that point, I'd spent a ton of time researching. I'd watched YouTube videos and online stalked people, such as Steve Scott, that I was so ready to take action but not sure what that looked like. Until I saw the webinar, that is. Chandler's big smile and Southern drawl had me hooked and James was such a goofball. I knew that I had found the right people to help me on this journey.

I was one of the first to apply to be one of their students on their new course, Self-Publishing School. I remember getting a phone call the next day from James. They'd read my application and felt I was a great fit for their coaching program… which cost US$3,000. After getting off the phone with James, I slumped in my chair. Here I was, a newly-wed still paying off the wedding and about to call my husband and ask (plead!) to spend another 5,000 New Zealand dollars that we didn't have on becoming an author, which he had no idea I was interested in pursuing. Needless to say, my husband is amazing! I joined Self-Publishing School and the rest, as they say, is history!

If you were deprived of all but one of your marketing tools, which would you keep and why?

I'd choose ConvertKit. It allows me to connect with my readers. It allows me to create landing pages that they host so that I can continue to build an email list. I'm able to distribute my books to my readers directly without having to worry about needing a distribution platform like Amazon. And the best part about all this is that I own that list. ConvertKit doesn't own it, I do. So, even if ConvertKit died, I'd still have my list. It's my No. 1 tool and I wouldn't trade it for anything!

What is an unusual habit that you have as a writer that helps you succeed?

For the past two years, I've been getting up at 4.30 a.m. As soon as I'm up, I aim to meditate for 10 minutes, then journal, if I feel called to do so, and then I have a drink of cold water. Then I'll get into my workout clothes and head off to do some exercise. By the time that's done and my husband has gone off to work, I'm sitting down to write at 8 a.m.

I make writing the first thing I do on my laptop. I don't check emails until I've completed this task. Nor do I respond to Facebook messages, or any other notifications that might pop up. My writing time is my No.1 priority, and it's sacred. Nothing else happens until I've completed at least an hour of writing.

The other thing that might be considered unusual is that I have all my positive affirmations set as reminders on my iPhone. They pop up throughout the day on my notifications screen, reminding me that I am a successful author, that I do deserve happiness, and that I should 'bring the joy' every day. It's like having a constant cheer squad in your face throughout the day.

What would you have done differently if you were to start your writing career with the knowledge you have now?

I'd start building an email list of my targeted readers.

I'd also have lined up my team earlier so that my production schedule ran like a well-oiled machine rather than a 1920s rusty old car like it did in the beginning.

I'd also have mapped out the next three years' writing schedule!

What bad advice do you often hear on the subject of self-publishing and book-marketing?

Here are the three most common things I hear that make me cringe when it comes to self-publishing and book marketing.

1. That you can get away with a cover design from Fiverr

Cover design is the most important aspect of a book's ability to sell, even more so than the words on the pages that follow. Cover design is where I spend the most amount of money because I know the difference it can make between a book that sells moderately and a book that sells well.

2. That you don't need to pay for an editor

This was advice I followed on my third book, *Side Hustle Blueprint: how to make an extra $1,000 writing ebooks*. I thought that after writing two books, I could get away without paying for an editor. A well-meaning online acquaintance told me that I didn't need to worry about an editor because he would read the book for me and let me know if he 'saw any issues'. Big mistake and the worst advice I have listened to. The book got slammed with 1-star reviews during launch week because there were so many errors that I had missed and so had my author friend. I quickly paid for an editor to revise it. Don't make that mistake. Always work with an editor.

3. That you should get your friends and family to review your books

This advice is something I still hear all the time. The problem with this is that firstly, you're in violation of Amazon's review policy and secondly, your friends and family are often *not* your target audience. That last part is important. You want

Amazon to do a lot of the heavy lifting during your launch period and the months that follow. And for Amazon to do its job well, you have to send your target reader to buy your book during your launch. If more friends and family buy your book vs. your target audience, Amazon has no idea who to share your book with. What will happen instead is that it will sink into rank oblivion never to be seen again.

What do you do when you feel demotivated or overwhelmed?

It's about changing my environment. I'll get up and go for a walk outside, head out to a coffee shop, or other similar space that allows me to write. If I'm feeling particularly demotivated, I'll crank up my dance music and have a mini-dance party in my office. And if I can't shake that feeling of being overwhelmed and demotivated, or of negativity, I'll close my laptop and instead watch something funny and light on Netflix.

Ultimately, I know that I'll have to sit with those feelings and let them wash over and through me and allow them to pass. I won't force myself to do anything I don't want to do, especially when it comes to writing.

What's your advice for authors who are still struggling?

You need to get some perspective, to take a step back and assess where you're at.

Step 1: If you're stuck, mind map!

If you're struggling with the writing part, then go back to mind mapping or brainstorming. I've found that when I'm stuck in my writing, it's often because I've a lot of ideas rolling around inside my head and unless I capture them, they'll continue to interrupt me. I'd recommend that when you're mind mapping, that you mind map your next six book ideas. If you've got more than that, mind map those too. Mind map until you can't mind map anymore!

Step 2: Have a writing mantra.

"Done is better than perfect!" This is my writing mantra. I'd hazard a guess that you're a bit of a perfectionist because most writers are. When it comes to our craft, we want to make sure it's just right before letting the world see it. But that often leads to our beautiful stories *never* getting published. And that is the worst thing we can do. We owe it to the world to share our gifts. What if your book was the one book that changed a person's life? How can you deny them that happiness? The best thing about being a self-published author is the ability to make changes to your published manuscript as often as you like. Nothing is set in stone. We live in a digital age.

So don't let the thought of imperfection stop you from hitting publish. Done *is* better than perfect.

Step 3: Put your business hat on.

A common theme I see in my coaching students is that they fail to think about their writing as a business. They want to make money as an author, yet they haven't considered what that looks like. And I get it. It's hard to think about this stuff when you're writing. If you want to make real money as an author, you'll have to take a step back, put on your business hat and approach your writing like it's a business — because it is. This means having a production schedule — a plan for how many books you're going to write in the next 12 months. You need to know how those books link to each other; how readers will connect with you further so that you can tell them about more of your books and products and/or services. It's about having a website, an email list, a plan to make it all happen. I know it sounds scary and overwhelming but you just take it one step at a time, just like you write your book one chapter at a time.

So, here's what you might need to think about:

1. What genre/niche you can write multiple books in
2. Who your target reader is
3. What products and/or services you could create further down the line
4. How many books you could write in a year
5. How you'll create a website
6. Which email platform you'll use
7. How you can leverage the author networks you already have.

Step 4: Decide who you want to serve the most.

This comes back to knowing who your target reader is and how you can serve them through your books, and later, products and services. One of the best ways to serve your readers and make money long-term is to create lead magnets (reader magnets) for them and start building your email list. Your email list will become your No.1 asset in your author business. With it, you've a direct connection to your readers and potential readers. Without it, you're completely disconnected from your readers. If the major platforms ever decided to change the rules for self-published authors, your email list and your ability to continue building it will be your saving grace. So, if you haven't started building your email list, do it *now*.

Step 5: Ask for help

Don't be afraid to seek advice. You might be alone in your writing, but you're not alone in the process. As self-published authors, we love to support each other. The world is big enough for us all to have a share in the pie. So don't struggle in silence. Find the right author community and be active. Connect with others and ask for help when you need it. We all need help every once in a while. And if you don't ask, you don't get the opportunity to get.

Step 6: Don't give up!

No matter where you are on your author journey, don't give up. You're just one book away from making it. If you give up, you will *never* achieve the success you dream about. Consistent action is what will get you there. This is the key difference between successful authors and unsuccessful authors. None of us were overnight successes. We all put in the hard work through consistently taking action.

Lise loves to help budding authors. She offers a variety of free and paid products and services. A good place to get started is her free resources vault (www.hustleandgroove.com/hustle-and-groove-vault). You'll find more free resources and links to courses and coaching programs on her website, www.hustleandgroove.com. You can also contact her at lise@hustleandgroove.com or connect with her on Instagram (www.instagram.com/lisecartwrightnz)

SALLY MILLER: By Constantly Researching, I Feel Closer to My Readers

Sally was another author I connected with because of this book. And I'm so glad I did!

Sally worked for 19 years as a project manager and business analyst in London and Silicon Valley. When her daughter was born, she discovered a new purpose. She left her corporate career to be a stay-at-home mom. She decided to find a way to stay home with her children and earn an income (without feeling torn between the two).

Sally is a self-confessed research geek and compulsive planner. She loves learning how stuff works, mastering new skills and sharing her knowledge with others. Her series of Make Money books include books on freelance writing, ghostwriting and self-publishing.

When did you start considering yourself financially successful as an author? How long did it take after you published your first book? How did it feel and why?

That was in 2016 when I reached my monthly income goal of $4,000 per month, working a 10-hour week. I'm also a stay-at-home mom and I'm fierce about protecting my family time. So I'd set myself a modest income goal and searched for ways to maximize my earnings from home. It was several years before I hit my initial income goal. At that time, I had multiple income streams including freelance writing, affiliate marketing, self-publishing and coaching.

It took even longer to realize the potential of self-publishing. It was late in 2017. I was reviewing my Amazon KDP reports and I looked at my lifetime earnings. I hadn't been focusing on my books. I'd simply let Amazon work its magic and keep selling my books for me. When I checked my lifetime earnings, I was pleasantly surprised to see that I'd earned more than $9,000 in book royalties. This income was entirely passive. I still didn't have an author platform. I wasn't doing anything to keep promoting my books after the initial launch.

My mind started ticking over… What if I had more books? What if instead of chasing shiny objects, I focused on writing? What if I built a platform for my books and started blogging about the same topics? How many more people could I help? How much more might I earn? Or to put it another way, what would happen if I focused on doing what I love and is already working?

This brings me to where I am today — publishing more books and building an author platform to promote my work.

It's an exciting journey. And it's thrilling to be doing work I love. Since deciding to focus on my books, I've seen a twofold increase in my book royalties. That's after just two months. I can't wait to see what happens next!

What have been the key factors to your success and why?

I believe there's one reason why my books sell well… even without ongoing promotion. It's because I write books that solve a pressing problem people are searching for on Amazon.

For example, my first book was *Make Money on Airbnb*. Airbnb is big news. People want to make money renting out their home or part of their home. My book gives them the exact steps to succeed as an Airbnb host. It has no fluff. It isn't a glorified sales letter for an expensive training course.

That is what people want: clear solutions to their problems. If you can deliver that, you will sell books.

What has been your worst decision as an entrepreneur and how did you bounce back and still get to where you are today? Did this failure set you up for your current success?

The worst thing I did was to overlook the potential of books for two years. I'm now correcting that mistake and focusing almost entirely on writing. But I can't help wondering where I'd be now if I'd come to this realization two years sooner.

Having said that, I'm grateful for everything I've done on my entrepreneurial journey. So, in that sense, the 'failure' did set me up for my current success. For example, I learned how to create online programs, build websites, connect with influencers, and garnered a host of other useful skills. I also gathered ideas for future books. I'm now leveraging this knowledge to grow my author platform, reach more readers and increase my author earnings.

It's tough to succeed as an author without also mastering online marketing. You may want to spend all your time writing. But on its own, writing great books won't make you successful. You also need to market your books, build a following and provide ongoing value to your readers.

Everything happens for a purpose. And while I may have taken many side paths to get to where I am today, each misstep has taught me something useful. The route to success isn't a straight line. And if it was, life wouldn't be any fun!

What has been your best decision as an author and why?

My best decision has been getting to know my readers. I truly care about my followers. I love hearing from them and want to help them succeed in life. I can spend an hour crafting a thoughtful reply to one person. Of course, I can't do this for everyone who reaches out to me. But I always seek to add value in the best way I can.

I believe that focusing on my readers helps me write better books. It also creates a strong connection between my followers and me. And it brings me deep work satisfaction. I write for a purpose — to help others like me make money from home and live a fulfilling life.

When you receive emails from your readers thanking you because you helped them through a difficult time in their life, or a message describing how you gave them hope, that is the greatest reward of all. As a writer, you change your readers' lives.

What is the best investment you've made as an author and why?

The best investment is time spent researching my readers' lives and looking for the best solution to solve their problems. I do this for every book I write. By constantly researching, I feel closer to my readers and it helps me write books that people want to buy.

The easiest (and most obvious) place to research a book idea is on Amazon. Here's how I start researching a book idea.

1. First, head over to Amazon and type a search term relating to your book topic into the search box. Make sure you also click the arrow on the left of the search box and select Kindle Store. This narrows your search to just the Kindle Store and not the entire Amazon platform.

2. Select 4-6 books in the same genre as the book topic. Try and find books with fewer than 20 reviews that aren't by big-name authors. This means you can easily compete with these books.

3. View the book pages for the 4-6 books you selected and find the overall ranking for each book. You can find this by scrolling down the Amazon book page to the Product Details area.

4. Make sure there are some books with a ranking less than 100,000 (No.1 is the highest-ranking book in the Kindle Store). A ranking below 100,000 means the author is selling at least one book a day.

5. If your first search is unpromising, repeat the process for related search terms. Keep going until you've identified a niche already selling in the Kindle Store.

The goal is to make sure there's an existing market for my book. If people are already buying books on a subject, then my book can sell too.

Once I have a viable book topic, I spend more time researching my idea. I look at questions and problems people ask in online forums. I read reviews and other books on the same subject. I'm looking for how I can write a book that people will want to buy and read. I want to add value to what's already out there.

If you were deprived of all but one of your marketing tools, which would you keep and why?

I'd keep my email list. My email subscribers are the first people to buy my books and write reviews. They share my books with their friends. And they inspire me to keep learning, writing and helping people.

What is an unusual habit that you have as an author that helps you succeed?

Like many authors, my most valuable habit is writing every day. It took me a while to master this habit. I tried lots of things and failed many times.

What eventually worked for me is somewhat unusual. Here's how I built a daily writing habit:

1. First, I set myself a tiny goal. I don't aim for 1,000 or 2,000 words per day. I simply tell myself to write for at least

30 minutes. Larger writing goals don't work for me. I find them intimidating and I put off writing altogether. Since setting my goal low, I write every day. Many days, I write for an hour or more.

2. Writing is the first thing I do each day. I used to check my emails first. But found that I'd get sucked into responding to other people's requests. The most important task in my business is writing. So I do this first. Everything else can wait.

3. Last of all, I only write in certain environments. I can't write in my office. The space doesn't inspire me. I either write in my bedroom or in a café.

What would you have done differently if you were to start your career with the knowledge you have now?

My entrepreneurial journey has been a winding road. I've made heaps of mistakes. Sometimes, I look back and wish I'd taken a straight line to success. But then I'd have missed out on many interesting diversions.

Having said that, if someone wants to avoid making the same mistakes I've made, I'd suggest they focus on one thing at a time. And give writing at least a year. It takes time to find your voice and the readers you want to write for.

It's also a good idea to start blogging before writing a book. That way you can experiment with shorter content. Discover what you love writing about and what your readers respond to. This also allows you to have an audience, however small, when you publish your first book.

What bad advice do you often hear on the subject of self-publishing and book-marketing?

This may sound like I'm contradicting one of my previous answers. But the worst advice I hear is to write for a market. Yes, you should research your market and write books that meet a need. So, in this sense I support writing to market. The problem with the write-to-market advice is that it ignores how important passion is. I believe everyone should do work they enjoy. When you tap into your gifts and write from your heart, you create great work. You write books your readers love. And you make a bigger impact in the world.

It drives me crazy when I see people ignoring their greatest gifts and passions. Each of us has a unique combination of strengths, experiences and interests. We owe it to the world to pursue our passions. By focusing on what makes us unique (and not looking at what others say we *should* be doing), we share our greatest gifts with the world.

What do you do when you feel demotivated or overwhelmed?

I walk or run outdoors. Being in nature and moving my body works wonders. I remember what matters most in my life and I find direction again.

I also journal, especially when I'm struggling to get clear about something. Writing freestyle helps me clarify my thoughts and let go of fear or a sense of being overwhelmed. When I buy a new journal, I write out my goals in the front of the journal. I read my goals every day. This reminds me of why I do my work and where I want to go.

Last (but most important), I play with my children. They are the reason I left my corporate job to work at home. I wanted more time with my children. My family brings me the most joy in life. And spending time with them never fails to ground me.

What's your advice for entrepreneurs who are still struggling?

First, embrace the journey. There's no such thing as an overnight success. And that's okay. Everything you do now is valuable. Whether it's a skill you learn or something you discover about yourself, you're not wasting your time. If you can keep your eye on the prize and be thankful for the present, you'll find success faster and have a lot more fun getting there.

Second, follow your passions. I believe happiness and success come from doing work you love. When you tap into your unique gifts and find a way to make what you do well about others, you create remarkable results.

Last of all, find your own path. It's easy to look at other people and think they have it all figured out. The truth is most people don't have it figured out (and probably aren't earning as much money as you think). Also what works for them might not work for you. This goes back to my previous point. Do what you love most and do best, not what other people say you should do.

You can find out more on Sally's website, www.sallyannmiller.com, where she writes about working from home and living your best life.

PART 6: TRANSFORMERS

CAITLIN PYLE: I Pretty Much Ignore Everyone Else

Now you're going to interview an entrepreneur who leveraged an aspect every writer needs to go through — proofreading! Caitlin created a successful proofreading course for writers and much more! She's truly amazing!

I was first approached by Caitlin to speak at her Work-At-Home Summit. I was excited to be part of the incredible lineup, and I was so impressed by how quickly she made me feel at ease. Caitlin throws some very high numbers she's making, but I think it's great — "If she can do it and she started at $30,000 a year," I ask myself, "why can't you?"

Caitlin began her work-at-home journey in 2011 after getting brutally fired from her $30,000-per-year corporate job. Starting with a freelance proofreading side hustle, Caitlin grew her freelance income to $40,000+ per year. Her business has since evolved into the multimillion-dollar media company it is today, and she's been featured in various notable media outlets such as Forbes.com, the *New York Post*, Business Insider, *Fast Company* and *Foundr*.

When did you start considering yourself financially successful as an entrepreneur?

I didn't consider myself financially successful as an entrepreneur until I saw my revenue each month consistently stay above $80,000. My business now generates multiple seven figures annually, and I *still* find myself worrying. As I spent much of my life believing I'd never earn more than $40,000 or so each year, it took me a while to condition my brain to calm down. I was earning more than I ever believed was possible for me but I'd got into the habit of buying only the cheapest things, wasting lots of time looking for coupons just to save a few dollars, and denying myself what I really wanted in the name of saving money. There's a big culture out there encouraging people to be 'satisfied' with less and accept their low-budget circumstances, and I want to speak out against that! If we want more money, there's no real reason why we shouldn't go out and earn it!

We have a lot of power to earn income. If we're willing to use our brains to learn skills that can solve problems for others, we will always be able to earn income. The more skills you have, the more problems you can solve and the more income you'll be able to earn!

I struggled a lot with the scarcity mindset, and I had quite a few people in my immediate sphere of influence who had many doubts because they knew nothing at all about information marketing or online business. All they knew was the corporate world, so they viewed building a business on the Internet as highly risky. I constantly got scarcity-mindset fueled questions like "What happens when you run out of people who are interested in what you have to say?" and comments like "Don't get too comfortable. Save all you can because you never know when the money will run out!"

How long did it take before you published your first piece of content? How did it feel and why?

It took me a week to publish my first piece of content, which was a 30-page ebook. I felt good about it but I knew it was far from perfect. I had no idea just how far from perfect it was at the time but that first ebook was the doorway into a lot of future success.

The initial feedback I got from the ebook wasn't that great; my first students had a lot of questions and a few people had complaints, which at first really irritated me. Then I got smart — their feedback was like free advice on how I could make my content better! When I shifted my mindset about that, I got to work on transforming my first ebook into my first online course, and I continued to implement all feedback I got on the course to make it better and better over time.

What have been the key factors to your success and why?

I've been successful because I've been consistent. I'm not always — hardly ever, actually! — the perfectly polished entrepreneur that incites envy on Instagram, but I'm consistent. I answer my emails. You can reach me. My students always tell me how refreshing it is to be able to contact me. That doesn't mean I'm able to spend the same amount of time on every email as I could in the beginning but being available and approachable on social media has played a major role in my success. It's easy to see I'm a real person — just like my prospective students/customers.

I also have a marketer's brain. I started my business knowing I wanted to make money. Many content creators start out trying to build an audience before they create a product. I did the opposite; I created a product and then created content to sell that product. The blog supported my product sales, added value to my brand and helped me gain trust.

A third factor in my success has been the avoidance of consuming too much content. I don't follow many blogs; I don't listen to any podcasts; I barely even read books, and if I do, it's only a few chapters until I've got enough to take action on. Normally, my to-do list is miles long at any given moment, so I don't see any point in consuming more information that will probably just overwhelm me, ignite a bout of comparisonitis, or worse. I like to say, somewhat jokingly, that I've become successful because I pretty much ignore everyone else. Hah!

What has been your worst decision as an entrepreneur and how did you bounce back and still get to where you are today? Did this failure set you up for your current success?

My worst decision as an entrepreneur was spending thousands of dollars to hire a consultant that forced me to spend a lot of time on stuff I don't feel mattered at all. She had come from a tech/software background, not information marketing, so doing all the traditional business stuff like writing a mission statement and coming up with a business plan seemed like a big waste of time to me. I'd rather spend the time coming up with strategy and execution plans.

Early on in my business, I also naively hired a 'consultant' for $2,200 per month and then an 'online business manager' for $1,500 a month. These people were self-glorifying virtual assistants, who were overcharging for the simplest tasks. Looking back, I kick myself for wasting the money. I don't like paying $75+ per hour for a meeting that consists mainly of me holding someone's hand and coming up with all the solutions myself.

What has been your best decision as an entrepreneur and why?

My best decision as an entrepreneur was to hire someone to help me answer emails. Because I was so keen on being available and approachable to my subscribers and prospective students, answering email quickly became the most time-consuming activity in my business — and it got to the point where by the time I was done answering emails, I had no energy left to do the big stuff that needed my attention. When I offloaded email responses to a virtual assistant, it freed me up to be creative and innovative in a way I couldn't be when I was spending all my time answering email!

What is the best investment you've made as an entrepreneur and why?

The best investment I've ever made as an entrepreneur has been my investment in sales funnels. In December 2016, I invested more than $20,000 to remodel the sales funnel for my flagship course on ProofreadAnywhere.com (PA). For the first 18 months of PA's existence, I had a simple email series plus a single sales page, then quite a clunky procedure in between to upsell students from one package to the next. The $20,000 investment included a ton of design, copy, video scripts and email integrations to streamline my entire process and automate the upsells.

A few months later, I worked with the same individual to create an automated webinar sales funnel for a second course on PA. We turned on the funnel in April 2017 and by January 2018, it had generated more than $1 million in evergreen sales — that's right; no launching!

If you were deprived of all but one of your marketing tools, which would you keep and why?

If I could only keep one marketing tool, it would be my email marketing software, ConvertKit. You can do so much cool stuff with it and it's so simple to use. My business generates a lot of revenue from email alone. For several months, I went through a phase where I didn't even publish any blog content; I only wrote emails — and I saw my sales go up!

What is an unusual habit that you have as an entrepreneur that helps you succeed?

I don't read many self-help books or blogs; almost none. I find most advice to be distracting and I only go looking for it when I really need it — not just because someone says I should read this book. I usually have a laundry list about a mile long of ideas and things I need to implement in my business, so until that list is empty, I don't see any real need to consume more content.

I suppose an unusual habit I have is simply not having habits. I don't do well with rituals or routine — eating the same thing all the time, doing the same workouts all the time... not my cup of tea.

What would you have done differently if you were to start your career with the knowledge you have now?

I'd have invested in tech virtual assistance and a higher-quality website far sooner than I did. At the beginning of my business, I struggled with the scarcity mindset big time. I was afraid to 'spend' money on my business because I feared I wouldn't earn it back. Now I realize that I wasn't spending money at all; I was investing it — and that I've total control over how much income I earn.

What bad advice do you often hear on the subject of online business and marketing?

Terrible advice? Build it and they will come. This just isn't true. You can build the most magnificent digital castle online, but if you don't create any pathways to it, it'll just get covered in weeds. When you're building something, you have to put yourself out there. I get asked all the time if putting yourself out there is necessary to grow a business, and my answer is always "Yes". It is! Putting yourself out there — otherwise known as marketing! — is a skill just like anything else and when you learn that skill, it becomes far less intimidating.

I was once told that my Facebook ads wouldn't work and that I *had* to do live webinars if I wanted to be successful. Four million dollars later, I still haven't done a single live webinar for my core products.

Lastly, people who say — or even believe! — you have to have a large social media following in order to make money are just crazy. I've a very modest social media following but a large and exceptionally responsive email list, plus great products.

What do you do when you feel demotivated or overwhelmed?

When I feel unmotivated or overwhelmed, I make a deal with myself. If I'm dreading something, such as my inbox, I'll set aside 30 minutes and challenge myself to get as many emails sorted as possible in that 30-minute block. When the 30 minutes have passed, I'm done — or at least I can quit if I want to. But what usually happens is I get some momentum! Not surprising since you get momentum only when you start moving… and many people wait for 'momentum' before they've even started moving at all!

I do something similar when I need to clean up my office or any other task I'm dreading. Just turn it into a game: how much I can get done in 10 minutes.

If I'm going through a longer phase of lack of motivation, I still make deals with myself. I determine what task I need to do to make the day a win. I call it my 'bare-ass minimum' — the thing I can do that will move things forward enough that I can feel good about it. I give myself permission to quit when I've done the task too — no guilt! Sometimes I'll get even more done than I bargained for. That makes me feel great!

What's your advice for entrepreneurs who are still struggling?

Don't copy others or spend too long consuming content. Work at being truly you in your branding, writing, social media — everything. It's so much easier to be you than it is to be somebody else, even if they're super successful and you want to be like them!

Secrets of Successful Authors and Publishers

It's easy to get stuck in the vortex of research and learning, where you spend tons of time thinking and planning but almost no time *doing*. The more time you spend *doing* things to grow your business — no matter how small — the more confidence you'll get. You'll be learning new things forever and ever but the learning curve is always steepest at the beginning. If you can get over the hard stuff at the beginning without quitting, as so many people do, you'll be on your way to success!

You can connect with Caitlin at www.caitlinpyle.co or look her up on Facebook.

CHRISTINE KLOSER:
What Was Missing Was Me

I met Christine at the Las Vegas mastermind thrown by Jesse Krieger, a mutual friend. Then we met again when we both spoke at Jesse's Bestseller Summit Live in Los Angeles. Now we can't stop inviting each other to each other's ventures!

Christine has a truly outstanding biography. Since 2004, she has trained nearly 70,000 entrepreneurs, leaders and authors to write their transformational books through her popular programs, Get Your Book Done®, the Transformational Author Experience®, Breakthrough LIVE and the My Time to Write® mentorship program. She's well recognized as the leader of the transformational author movement, and is gifted at helping her clients feel seen, heard, valued and understood in ways that transform their lives, books and businesses. Her passion is to help people liberate their message — so they can *be* who they were born to be and *do* what they are here to do! Many of her clients have gone on to become bestselling authors, sign traditional publishing contracts, speak around the world and appear in major media, including CNBC, CBS, *Time, BusinessWeek*, CNN, ABC, *The New York Times* and TEDx.

When did you start considering yourself financially successful as an author? How long did it take after publishing your first book? How did it feel, and why?

I wrote a book called *The Freedom Formula: how to put soul in your business and money in your bank* in 2008 and it was an immediate success. It was endorsed by top thought leaders, such as Arielle Ford, Michael Gerber, Mark Victor Hansen, Loral Langemeier and Neale Donald Walsch. It won awards and became a bestseller on Amazon — not just in some obscure subcategory but in the overall Top 100 books on Amazon.

I leveraged that book to sell out my first three-day seminar and generated half a million dollars in new revenue at that event. This all happened within six months of the book being published. This all sounds great, right? It's every author's dream! So, there I was with this external financial success…

But I was miserable. And it quickly dawned on me. What I had done was created a business around that book that was simply not aligned with my purpose and values.

What were the key factors in your success, and why?

One key factor in writing *The Freedom Formula* and having the ability to sell more than $500,000 in coaching and masterminds was I had already built up a huge network of women entrepreneurs from scratch over a period of eight years in Los Angeles, where I founded the Network for Empowering Women Entrepreneurs. Another was that I spent a powerful — and long — day at the spa reflecting on why I was writing the book, who I was writing it for, how to write it and what kind of message I wanted to deliver to the world. Getting away from my usual environment is a big deal for me. This is how you can get clear on your message before you write a single word in your book.

What was your worst decision as a writer? How did you bounce back and still get to where you are today? Did this failure set you up for your current success?

After I wrote *The Freedom Formula*, I closed $500,000 in business in three days. It was a huge financial success. But it was a gigantic personal failure because I started saying "Yes" to a lot of things that didn't feel totally aligned. I said "Yes" to coaching some clients and shouldn't have. And soon afterwards I knew in my heart something was terribly wrong. Everything felt 'off' to me. There were days when I just couldn't get out of bed. I stayed in my bathrobe feeling depressed and trying to figure out what went wrong; what didn't work; how all that so-called success could actually leave me with a business I didn't want. It was the wrong business. I had some incredibly challenging clients and I woke up with this feeling of dread almost every day.

Saying "Yes" to the wrong things too quickly was the worst decision I made as an author. It's difficult to say "No" after your first formidable success. Unfortunately, I just didn't have the right coach to help me dig deeper and ask the tough questions before I made the choices that led to building the wrong business.

I knew I was at a critical choice point. I could either bite the bullet and just buck up and keep going no matter how terrible or wrong it felt — or I could let everything go, shut down my business, suffer the financial ramifications and figure out what the heck wasn't working.

What was your best decision as an author and why?

As gut-wrenching as the decision was, I chose to shut down that first business I built. I let everything go. I processed a lot of refunds and I was back to ground zero. When you have money, you quickly realize that money isn't everything and the wrong kind of money can bring a lot of misery into your life. That's what happened to me.

As painful as that decision was, it became the best decision I could possibly have made. I went through months of meditation, prayer, reading, reflection, writing in my journal and figuring out what went wrong. In that difficult period, I created an author's tool that would change everything! Once I put it into action, it helped me build up my business again, this time to $1.2 million in revenue within a few years, while *also* being happy about it and loving my work and my clients.

What is the best investment you've made as an author, and why?

For four months I was even *more* miserable than I had been when I had clients I didn't want and a business I wasn't aligned with. I felt lost and scared. I woke up at 5 a.m. every morning and meditated and prayed for two hours. I wanted to know that all this pain, doubt and confusion I was going through meant something. I prayed, begged and bargained with God to show me why I was experiencing such difficulty and how I could use it to serve and help others. And I did discover what had been missing in my last business. I had the money stuff figured out. I charged high fees and people were happy to pay me. I had a message that resonated with clients. *The Freedom Formula* was and still is a great book that impacts entrepreneurs all over the world. But what was missing was *me*!

That's when I realized that writing a book and building a business isn't just about money, your customers and impacting the world. Those are important things but you also have to look at it holistically and figure out if the person beneath it all — the author and entrepreneur — is fully aligned with the message.

This is when I discovered the first iteration of the Transformation Quadrant concept. This is a tool that can help you see your book and its purpose from a holistic point of view. When you write a book, you're not just changing your readers' lives, growing your business and impacting the world; you're transforming yourself as an author and a human being! Once I understood these four quadrants of a book-based business, I joyfully built up my business again into something I love and am passionate about to this day. The investment of time and energy in my personal transformation was what changed my life and business in the most magnificent way. It wasn't easy but I'm grateful I did it.

If anyone ever tells you you can't have it all, take it from me they're wrong. You can!

If you were deprived of all your marketing tools and could keep only one, which would it be, and why?

I'd keep joint-venture partnerships — groups of friends and colleagues who also have audiences and support each other's business goals. For example, this very book you're holding in your hands was co-authored by joint-venture partners working together to help you, and support our messages getting out in the world.

And it's not just authors and online marketers who do this. When actors have a new movie to promote, they go on talk shows with large audiences to promote it. When authors launch new books, they do podcast tours, which are versions of joint ventures that help you get your message in front of people who might not know you yet.

If I were being cheeky, I'd say that the one marketing tool I'd keep is my ability to make friends. Connecting with people is a powerful skill that everyone needs in order to succeed.

What unusual habit do you have that helps you succeed as a writer?

I go to the spa! I'm not joking. That's where my biggest business breakthroughs happen. All I need is one full day of being unplugged (and getting a facial or massage) to gain crystal clarity on my next book, program or product. In fact, my signature program for authors, "Get Your Book Done", was entirely created sitting by the indoor pool at the spa at The Hotel Hershey. I can't emphasize enough how important it is to give yourself time to reflect, meditate and create in a distraction-free zone.

I truly believe that changing your environment is a necessity, especially for authors. It's nice to think you can write at home or sneak in an hour at work or whatever, but sometimes you just need to get away to focus fully and crank up your creativity. That's why I host five transformational writing retreats a year — to give my author clients time and space away from everyday life to write.

Go to a cafe. Go to the library. Go to a relative's house if they don't mind. When you're at home or somewhere familiar, you go into a monotonous routine, and that can carry over into your writing. I'm not saying you can't write without doing this but it's hard for most people.

What would you have done differently if you had begun your writing career with the knowledge you have now?

I would've properly developed my Transformation Quadrant concept before I wrote a single word of my book. I'd have dug into each quadrant to gain clarity on it individually as well as how they worked together to create holistic success for me, my readers, my business and the world.

It's not fun to write the wrong book and build the wrong business. In fact, it's downright miserable. But that can happen if you move too fast without having a solid four-pronged foundation upon which to build.

What bad advice do you often hear on the subject of self-publishing and book-marketing?

The worst advice I hear suggests you can write your book in just a couple of days. People who advocate using this 'microwave method' of book-writing are selling authors short. Most well-known and respected *New York Times* bestselling authors will tell you it took a few years to write their book. They'll tell you that writing is a process that evolves over time and that cranking out a book too fast compromises depth and quality, two things essential for longevity as a successful author.

Here's an example. At a conference a few years ago, I connected with a yoga teacher who was excited about her new book. But in the middle of our conversation, she broke down and started crying. As she talked more deeply, she realized she had written the wrong book — one that didn't connect with the future she wanted to create for herself, her readers or her business. She had worked with a coach who taught her the 'microwave method' and it was the worst thing she could have done.

What do you do when you feel unmotivated or overwhelmed?

I go to the spa regularly to solve my writing and business challenges but it's really about self-reflection time. I know the answers are already inside me and will come from the quiet contemplation and connection to God. This is why I spend one hour, six days a week, in quiet contemplation. It stops me from feeling overwhelmed and helps me to counter confusion and any other challenge I face.

What's your advice for authors who are still struggling?

In my experience coaching tens of thousands of authors since 2004, it comes down to developing your Transformation Quadrant profile and going back to it over and over again as you write. Once that is clear and you know what your book's purpose is in all four quadrants (self, reader, business and world), you can never lose your way. It's like the GPS for your book. You simply don't struggle anymore. You know your 'big why'; you know how your message will impact lives. You're motivated to finish your book so you can grow your business. And most important, you're confident that you're writing the right book for the right reasons and you're headed in the right direction!

Secrets of Successful Authors and Publishers

You have no more excuses. If you're not writing and moving forward, it's probably because your Transformation Quadrant profile is out of alignment with your true goals and purpose. It's that simple.

Christine invites you to take her deep-dive webinar training. This training typically costs $297 but since you are a *Write and Grow Rich* reader, she'll share it with you for free. Visit her website www.christinekloser.com/write-and-grow. She'll show you how to build your Transformation Quadrant profile step by step. It's a 70-minute course and worth every minute! If you have questions, just reach out to info@christinekloser.com.

JASON LADD: Follow the Meaning

I was first introduced to Jason by a mutual friend. Jason shows you that you can be a successful author no matter where you live — even in Alaska!

He's helped many authors get reviews for their books with his Book Review Banzai method.

Jason is a bestselling author and book review expert who served for 14 years on active duty with the U.S. Marines. Before publishing the award-winning *One of the Few*, he flew as an instructor pilot in the F/A-18 "Hornet" and the F-16 "Fighting Falcon". Jason is the creator of Indielisters (a service that helps authors choose effective book promotion services) and the architect of Book Review Banzai, a technique for planning and launching successful book-review campaigns. He writes from a cabin in Alaska and enjoys photography, using chainsaws and playing hockey with his children on their outdoor rink. He and his wife Karry are the parents of seven children.

When did you start considering yourself financially successful as an author? How long did it take after you published your first book? How did it feel and why?

I haven't hit my goals for what I'd consider to be financial success but that doesn't mean I haven't hit other goals, and it doesn't mean that I'll stop writing any time soon. Every author has their own path, each with twists and turns they might never have expected. I often repeat a mantra related to this topic — "Don't follow the money. Follow the meaning." When you follow the meaning, you'll be far more fulfilled than if you follow the money. And when you're doing what you love and what you believe is important, the money might even follow.

What have been the key factors to your success and why?

For me, it's been important to keep an eternal perspective which includes prioritizing faith and family above all. Having an eternal perspective keeps you from taking yourself too seriously. It prevents you from burnout and frustration. It gives you the freedom to stop and breathe when things aren't going your way with your writing. In the long run, keeping this mindset allows you to re-energize and re-engage with new vitality.

What has been your worst decision as a writer and how did you bounce back and still get to where you are today? Did this failure set you up for your current success?

My worst decision so far has been to publish a book that could have been better. As I gained knowledge about the writing process, I realized that my first book was too ambitious. It covered too many topics and lacked, therefore, the focus readers expect. But I was several years into the book and suffering from getitpublisheditis!

Even though I view this as a mistake, it did yield some benefits. The time that would have been spent improving the book was instead spent learning how to market and promote. And sometimes the benefits of moving on can outweigh the benefits of getting bogged down!

Could I have made the book better? I think so. Would it have made a significant difference? I'm not so sure. It's still a good book, and instead of a prolonged bout of perfectionism, I was able to learn faster about post-publication processes.

What has been your best decision as an author and why?

My best decision was to take a year off after publishing my first book in order to learn marketing and promotion. My initial launch was disappointing. I didn't get the sales or reviews I was hoping for. I figured out how to drive downloads — enough to hit No.1 on Amazon in several free and paid categories — but that didn't lead to anything. I wasn't able to secure the bigger promotions because I was an indie author with a single book and a low review count.

During a promotion for *One of the Few*, I created the database that would become Indielisters, a service that now helps indie authors find effective book promotion services. And repeated BookBub 'Featured Deal' rejections were the impetus behind developing the Book Review Banzai technique, a method that teaches authors how to launch successful book-review campaigns.

What is the best investment you've made as an author and why?

The best investment you can make as an author is in experiences. There's a reason that I didn't become an author until later in life. Before my writing career, I spent time with the Marines, learned how to be a fighter pilot, and provided air support to men and women on the ground in combat. I've also been raising a family. We've had great times and we've endured times of pain and suffering. It's because of these experiences that I can relate to others better.

But more important than the experiences is the perspective. We continue to acknowledge that we don't know what we don't know, and with that comes a humility that can soften the hardest of hearts. Ultimately, we write to connect; with experiences and perspective, your connections will run deep. Drawing on experiences, you can write about what you know and what you know will help others.

If you were deprived of all but one of your marketing tools, which would you keep and why?

I'm a huge fan of GMass, a Google Chrome extension that works with your Gmail account. It's a mail merge program that allows you to send individual one-on-one emails in bulk and is perfect for making initial connections with influencers or book-review candidates. GMass is best used as a supplement to your list management service (MailChimp, ConvertKit, etc.).

GMass has powerful features including auto follow-up options, automatic first-name detection (based on email address) and the ability to send on a timeline or even space out your emails. Another standout feature of GMass is their reputation for deliverability. After reading a few posts on the GMass blog, users can learn how to ensure their emails end up in the inbox (and primary tab if the recipient is using Gmail and tabs) instead of the spam or promotions folder.

GMass is also one of the most affordable services out there. They have a free option and their most expensive plan is less than $13 per month. Regarding both deliverability and open rates, nothing has worked better than GMass when I've run comparisons.

What is an unusual habit that you have as a writer that helps you succeed?

I often have my writing reviewed by my family before I publish. They're like a pretentiousness/loquaciousness death squad. In other words, they'll call me out if I start throwing in 50-cent words to explain a two-cent topic. They've taught me that effective writing is not only about finding the perfect words but also about how perfectly you've tapped into a reader's experience. Smart writers don't try to sound smart. They keep it clear and compelling.

What would you have done differently if you were to start your writing career with the knowledge you have now?

I'd have kept my first nonfiction book short. The first draft was around 90,000 words. The only reason it was that long was because I had a friend who published a book that was around that size. That's a terrible reason to write a long book. My second book was only 50 pages because that was sufficient to accomplish the purpose of the book (to introduce the book-review campaign planning process to as many authors as possible).

Writing a fiction book might be different. If your goal is to captivate your reader with a 400-page epic fantasy, then longer might be more appropriate. But for nonfiction, you want to get them in and keep them moving. Readers like to progress through a nonfiction book and they feel good after completing each chapter. So keep them short — no more than around 2,000 words per chapter is a good goal. There are always exceptions based on your book's topic but shorter is usually better.

What bad advice do you often hear on the subject of self-publishing and book-marketing?

The worst advice an author could receive on the topic of self-publishing is to avoid self-publishing. Self-publishing is a rapidly evolving industry and shows no signs of slowing any time soon. Every year, new tools and services make self-publishing easier, faster and more enticing. The allure of having a book traditionally published remains for many, and depending on your goals, that might be the route for you. But if it doesn't work out, then that's no reason to become discouraged. Ultimately, your success will be based on the words you imprint upon the reader, not the imprint the reader sees on the spine.

Regarding book marketing, one of the biggest challenges to authors is getting social proof for their book in the form of book reviews. The worst advice I've heard to get more book reviews is to get more downloads and sales for their book. This is a chicken-and-egg problem. The goal of many authors is to increase revenue. To get sales, you need reviews. But you can't get reviews without sales. (Or can you?) So what's an author to do? Some authors are told that it's a numbers game, and if they can get enough downloads of their ebook, they'll start getting reviews. This is a half-truth. It's a numbers game. The problem is that going with the 'get a massive amount of downloads' method doesn't get you the numbers you need.

Mark Dawson is a multiple *USA Today* bestselling author with more than 20 books and more than 2 million books downloaded worldwide. In his Self-Publishing Formula podcast episode, "How to Get Reviews", he estimates that an author might expect to receive one review for every 1,000 sales. And in the case of a free download, you might expect one review for every 5,000-10,000 downloads. That means that if a book promotion site requires you to have 10 book reviews to book a promotion, you might need 10,000 sales or up to 100,000 free downloads. A solution to this problem is to conduct a proper book launch with an advance reader team or 'street team'. The challenge here is figuring how to build one big enough to move the needle on reviews. I call this launching a book-review campaign and it has been an area of focus for me over the last few years. The secret is connecting with a large number of people willing to receive your ebook for free and who will consider leaving a review. Plan on 30 percent of your team actually coming through with a review.

What do you do when you feel demotivated or overwhelmed?

When I'm demotivated, I need music, mostly big-arrangement soundtracks. We're talking Hans Zimmer, James Horner, Steve Jablonsky stuff. If I need to think, I'll put on "Mountains" from *Interstellar*. If I need to feel a sense of growth and transformation, I'll go with "Battle Room" from *Ender's Game*. If I'm dying to feel a sense of purpose, I need "In the beginning" from *The Bible*.

When I'm overwhelmed, I have to stop. I'll go for a run or work on a project around the house. Sometimes you need to clear your head, and sometimes it feels like you're wasting your time. I believe there are two things that are never a waste of time — strengthening your body with exercise, and strengthening your mind and soul with Scripture. So I'll do one or both to feel better, and then return to the task at hand. It usually works.

What's your advice for authors who are still struggling?

Embrace it. It's part of the process. This is easy for me because Marines believe glory is derived through suffering. And what a glorious thing it is to be a writer! You can make it less prolonged but you cannot avoid it completely. All authors struggle but you won't struggle forever. The struggle will become a groove and when you're in the groove, you have the potential to write and grow rich!

You can learn more about Jason at www.jasonbladd.com

STEVE ALCORN: I Try to Make Each Word Count

I was introduced to Steve by a mutual friend and we've been supporting one another ever since.

Steve is the CEO of Alcorn McBride Inc., a company that designs products used in nearly all of the world's theme parks.

He's the author of many books, including historical fiction, romance, young adult novels and many nonfiction books including *How to Fix Your Novel*, *Building a Better Mouse* and *Theme Park Design*. As the founder of Writing Academy, Steve has helped more than 30,000 aspiring authors structure their novels through the online learning programs of 2,000 colleges and universities worldwide.

When did you start considering yourself financially successful as an author? How long did it take after you published your first book? How did it feel and why?

In 1982, I was part of the design team that created Walt Disney World's Epcot. Shortly after that, a co-worker and I began writing a book about the experience, *Building a Better Mouse: the story of the electronic engineers who built Epcot*. But life got in the way and we didn't finish it. I founded Alcorn McBride, the company that designs the audio and video products used throughout the world's theme parks.

It was 20 years later when I got back to *Building a Better Mouse*. It was a good thing we had written most of the book right after the project because when I returned to the manuscript, I hardly remembered most of the stories! I finished it and published it. It was an immediate hit because the market was ripe for it — an important lesson. In the meantime, I had been studying writing and had published three novels. But *Building a Better Mouse* was the first big success.

I then put all that learning to work and began creating writing classes for Writing Academy and books about how to write, both of which were also immediately successful. So, it took 20 years of work to become a successful author, but in another sense, it happened overnight. And of course, it was very gratifying.

What have been the key factors to your success and why?

Most of my bestselling books are nonfiction. They are books about the theme park industry and 'how to' books for writers. Their success is due to my activity in both those industries. That's part of the marketing process. Because I'm still actively involved in the theme park industry, and because I teach thousands of students how to structure their writing every year, my books are constantly exposed to readers who are interested in their subject matter.

Secrets of Successful Authors and Publishers

As an author, you may not think of yourself as a marketer, but in fact most of the time we authors spend is on marketing our books. Even traditionally published authors are now expected to do their own marketing because publishers can no longer afford to publicize the vast majority of new books. As they can no longer rely on simply putting their products on bookstore shelves, they've pushed the marketing efforts of most books onto the authors themselves. But if you're going to be doing all the marketing, why not make all the profit? You'll earn 10 times as much per copy selling your self-published book. And your book will remain in print forever, rather than spending a few months on bookstore shelves and then being remaindered.

This is perhaps the single most important factor in building wealth through writing. My book *Building a Better Mouse* has been selling well since the day it was published almost 20 years ago, and it will continue to sell well in the future.

The trick to selling books is getting good reviews on Amazon so your book pops the top of searches. There are many approaches to getting good reviews, and whole classes are devoted to the subject. But at its root, the single most important aspect of getting a good review is writing a great book.

My advice is to start by arming yourself with the best information you can about what goes into a novel, a memoir or a work of nonfiction. That means reading or taking classes about story structuring, manuscript writing and editing.

What has been your worst decision as a writer and how did you bounce back and still get to where you are today? Did this failure set you up for your current success?

The worst decision I ever made as a writer was to put off publishing that first book for nearly 20 years! On the other hand, technology caught up with me and allowed me to self-publish, which proved far more lucrative than if I'd signed a publishing contract 20 years earlier. Had I done the latter, the book would now be long out of print. Instead, it continues to generate royalties every month.

What has been your best decision as an author and why?

My best decision as an author and teacher has been to focus on structure. Whether writing fiction or nonfiction, focusing on the structure up front is essential to success. This is what I teach in all of my classes, and I practice it in all of my books.

I also try to make sure I'm providing valuable content. Whether in a book, an email to my followers, a post on Facebook or a writing class, I try to make each word count. There is no substitute for great content.

What is the best investment you've made as an author and why?

It doesn't require a lot of money to become a successful author. But it does require a lot of time. Much of that time is spent in writing the book, and even more of it is spent in marketing the book. But the most important time is spent learning how to make that book great. The 20 years I spent studying story structure and the subtle aspects of fiction are the best investment I ever made.

If you were deprived of all but one of your marketing tools, which would you keep and why?

There are lots of ways to market your book, with various levels of return on invested cost and time. They include working a mailing list, providing content for online blogs, and sending out review copies. But the single best marketing tool is the blurb you use to describe your book on Amazon. It's worth analyzing every single word and especially the opening sentence of that description, because if you don't grab readers in those first few seconds, you've lost the sale.

What is an unusual habit that you have as a writer that helps you succeed?

I make extensive use of voice dictation when I write. I've used it to write all of my fiction and nonfiction books. And I've used it to create all of my written classes.

It helps that I have a lot of practice in public speaking, and I have a lot of practice recording videos. Very little editing of the transcribed copy is needed. It allows me to get my thoughts down with a natural flow and in a natural voice.

I often dictate late at night, when the house is quiet and I can focus without interruption. If you haven't tried voice-transcription software, or if you haven't tried it lately, you'll be surprised how it has improved over the last 20 years.

What would you have done differently if you were to start your writing career with the knowledge you have now?

I'd have started sooner and would have published even more books by now. On the other hand, because of the time frame when I began publishing books, I hit the perfect window for the self-publishing world, and this has led to my publishing efforts being very profitable, and ongoing. So perhaps it's just as well I waited until I did.

What bad advice do you often hear on the subject of self-publishing and book-marketing?

The worst advice I've heard about self-publishing is that you can do everything yourself. You can't produce your best work in a vacuum. Yes, there are techniques you can use to see your own work with fresh eyes, such as reading the pages backwards, setting them aside for a few months and then revisiting them. But the fact is you can't have a bestselling self-published book unless it's of professional quality, and all professionals use editors in order to check their work. If your book has not been professionally edited and proofread, it's probably not going to become a bestseller.

Furthermore, if your book hasn't been planned out in advance before you even started writing, it's probably not well enough structured to be successful. You owe it to yourself to educate yourself through reading books about writing and taking classes about writing so you can produce your very best work.

The worst advice I hear about marketing is that you can rely upon an email list to do all your marketing for you. It helps to have a great email list, but building a giant email list of people who aren't really interested in your subject matter is useless and expensive. And abusing the people who are on your email list with piles of advertising isn't productive either. I'm very careful with my list to make sure all my emails contain valuable content for my followers.

What do you do when you feel demotivated or overwhelmed?

I love to be busy, so I'm seldom demotivated or overwhelmed. When I want to write about a subject, I research it by listening to other books on that subject. That includes writing novels. I love to research settings and historical information by reading other fiction set in the time or place my book will be set.

I find all reading inspirational. I enjoy both nonfiction and fiction books, and do most of my reading using audiobooks during my commute to and from work, and during airplane flights. I find the audiobook experience to be nearly identical to traditional reading, and after a few months I usually can't remember whether I read or listened to a given book.

What's your advice for authors who are still struggling?

Do not give up. Giving up is a guaranteed way to fail. That's easy to say, harder to do. Motivate yourself by listening to or reading books you love. Make sure you're passionate about your subject. And work to a plan. If you don't have a solid plan, you can't succeed.

Even if you started a manuscript and got stuck, it's not too late to go back and structure. Your book will go through many drafts, so it doesn't matter if you set aside already-written material and start again. Perhaps you'll find a place for it, perhaps not. Don't be afraid to start over if you've stalled.

Taking a class at Writing Academy is a great way to make sure you have a solid foundation upon which to build. With that foundation in place, you're guaranteed to succeed.

> To explore Steve's books, visit his website at
> www.themeperks.com

> To start structuring your book today, visit
> www.writingacademy.com. There are classes on writing
> fiction or nonfiction, and there are very attractive monthly
> subscriptions.

ASH AKSHAY GOEL AND SUSMITA DUTTA: Your Branded UFO, From Author to Authority

Ash Akshay Goel is a certified business growth consultant, book marketing specialist, and an international bestselling author. He has a track record of helping numerous six-figure and seven-figure businesses grow exponentially with the help of "Book Funnels." Renowned for his expertise in AI/automation, funnel hacking, and growth strategies, Ash has been a sought-after keynote speaker and an IIT-IIM graduate. To learn more about Ash and how he can help you grow your business by building done-for-you book funnels, email him at ash@globalbookpublishing.com.

Susmita Dutta, as the CEO of Global Book Publishing, plays a pivotal role in the literary world, guiding authors to bestseller status. She runs a unique publishing house, where she offers 100% copyrights, 100% control, and 100% reach to the authors. She has helped more than 110 authors share their stories with the world. She focuses on two book types: (a) Love and Legacy books and (b) Brand and Business books. Her influence extends to being a leading educator on Udemy and Learn @ Forbes, with more than 230,000+ global enrollments on Udemy. To learn more about Sush, Global Book Publishing, and how they can help you write an international bestselling book, even if you have no time, no expertise, and no publishing experience, visit https://globalbookpublishing.com or email at support@globalbookpublishing.com.

Imagine being in a crowded, noisy room where everyone is talking at once. The air is filled with chatter, and it feels like you're trying to speak, but no one can hear you. The lights are low, making it hard to see clearly, and the pressure to get noticed is overwhelming. This is how it feels like to brand yourself in today's busy market. It's frustrating and exhausting, isn't it?

But what if you had a secret weapon? Something that could make you rise above the noise, helping you command attention and respect? That's exactly what a Branded UFO can do for you.

So, what's a UFO? No, we're not talking about little green men or flying saucers. We're talking about a Unique Framework Offering (UFO) that can launch your brand and transform you from just another face in the crowd into a respected authority in your industry.

Our UFO Journey: From Struggling Experts to Soaring Authorities

We're Ash Akshay Goel and Sush Dutta, and we want to share how creating our own UFOs changed everything for us.

Picture this: We were a dynamic duo full of energy and passion, ready to help people write and publish their bestselling books. We had the skills, the experience, and the motivation to really make a difference. But something wasn't working. Despite our relentless efforts, we were getting lost in the overwhelming crowd, becoming just another voice in the noisy, chaotic marketplace.

We tried everything but nothing seemed to work. We attended countless conferences, lugging our suitcases from one city to the next. We invested heavily in marketing, from Facebook ads to hiring "experts" who promised us the world. We engaged online tirelessly, answering questions, sharing insights, and doing all the "right" things.

And what did we have to show for it? A few sales, a lot of exhaustion, and a growing sense of frustration.

Then, BAM! The moment came that changed everything.

We were at yet another conference, feeling a bit defeated and wondering if we should just throw in the towel. That's when we stumbled upon the idea of a Branded UFO while attending a talk by Russell Brunson. Little did we know that this was about to be our "aha" moment.

Russell talked about the importance of creating a unique identity. He explained how distilling your expertise into a memorable, easy-to-understand framework could skyrocket your authority and make your offer irresistible. It was a revelation.

As we listened, it was like a light bulb went off. We realized we had been so focused on what we were offering that we had neglected how we presented it. We didn't have a clear, compelling framework that set us apart and made our expertise tangible.

Right there, in that big conference hall, we started scribbling ideas. By the time we landed back home, we had the beginnings of not one, but two transformative frameworks.

The first was the **P3 Program: Personalized Partnership Publishing Program**. This framework captured our unique approach: working hand-in-hand with authors, tailoring our support to their individual needs, and treating the publishing process as a true partnership.

We didn't stop there. We also developed the **EPIC Publishing Path: Expert Publishing through Impactful Collaboration**. This framework laid out the step-by-step process we take our authors through, from the initial concept to the published book and beyond.

These weren't just catchy names or marketing gimmicks. They were true representations of our process and philosophy, packaged in a way that made them easy to understand and remember.

Once we had our frameworks in place, everything changed. We rewrote our website copy around these concepts. We restructured our talks and presentations to showcase our UFOs. We even redesigned our business cards to feature visual representations of our frameworks.

The results were nothing short of astronomical. Within 12 months, our business had grown tenfold. Yes, you read that right – 10x growth!

But it wasn't just about the numbers. The quality of our leads improved dramatically. Instead of us chasing potential clients, they started reaching out to us. And when they did, they weren't asking about generic book-writing services. They were specifically inquiring about our P3 Program and the EPIC Publishing Path.

We went from being just another book writing and publishing service to being THE go-to experts for authors who want a personalized, partnership-based approach to getting their books out into the world.

The Power of the Branded UFO

Our story isn't just luck. It shows how Branded UFO could transform our offering.

While creating unique frameworks that capture your expertise, follow the **MAGNET Framework**:

1. **M - Memorable**: Makes your solution easy to understand and remember.
2. **A - Authority**: Establishes you as an expert and a thought leader.

3. **G - Generates Buzz**: Gives people something specific to talk about, latch onto, and share with others.
4. **N - Niche Appeal**: Helps you be unique in the crowded marketplace.
5. **E - Engaging**: Captures attention and keeps your audience interested.
6. **T - Transformational**: Amplifies your impact and helps you achieve lasting change by spinning off the UFO into talks, courses, and more.

Your Branded UFO is more than just a marketing tool. It's a strategic asset that can propel your business to new heights.

Don't just take our word for it. Let's look at some real-world examples of Branded UFOs that have catapulted brands to the forefront of their industries:

- Simon Sinek's *Golden Circle*: His simple "Why, How, What" framework revolutionized how people think about leadership and marketing.
- Tony Robbins's *6 Human Needs*: It helps people understand the basic drivers of their behaviors and decisions.
- Stephen Covey's *7 Habits of Highly Effective People*: It became a popular numbered UFO in personal and professional development.
- Michael Porter's *Five Forces*: This model became the basis for teaching business strategy for analyzing competitive intensity and industry attractiveness.

These thought leaders didn't just write books. They created frameworks that made them authorities in their fields.

The Branded UFO Blueprint (BUFO)

Ready to embark on your journey to authority? Let's dive into the blueprint for crafting your own Branded UFO:

1. BUILD: Identify Your Unique Approach and Build Your Framework

First, dig deep. What makes your approach unique? What do you do differently from others in your field? What special skills, knowledge, or experiences do you bring to the table?

Don't be shy! This is your time to shine. Think about the problems you solve, the results you deliver, and the way you make people feel.

Talk to your clients or customers. What do they say makes you stand out? What keeps them coming back for more?

Then, you transform your brilliance into a structured, tangible offering. Think of it as the architectural plans for your authority empire.

Your framework could be a step-by-step process, a set of guiding principles, a visual model, or even a catchy acronym.

Remember, the goal is to simplify your expertise into a format that is easy for others to understand and remember.

Action Steps:

   a. List three to five things that make your approach unique.
   b. Sketch out your framework. Don't worry about perfection; focus on clarity.

2. **U**NIQUE IDENTITY: Name It to Claim It

A unique name can make all the difference. It should be catchy, memorable, and evoke the essence of your unique value.

Brainstorm words or phrases that capture your brand's personality and the transformation you offer.

Don't be afraid to get creative! A playful name can spark curiosity and make your framework more appealing. A great name can instantly make your framework memorable. Try to come up with something catchy but also descriptive of your work.

When naming your framework, consider using:

- Alliteration (like "The Four Fs of Financial Freedom")
- Numbers (like "The 5-Step Success System")
- Acronyms (like our P3 Program and EPIC Path)
- Metaphors and analogies

The goal is to create a name that is clear, attractive, and easy to remember. Test it out on friends or colleagues. If they can remember it easily, you're on the right track.

Action Step: Brainstorm five to ten potential unique names for your framework.

3. **F**LASHBACK FACTOR: Make it visual and increase the flashback factor.

A picture is worth a thousand words, and a well-designed visual can amplify the impact of your framework and make people remember it forever.

Think about making a diagram. It can be a flowchart or infographic. It should show your process or principles. A strong visual can make your framework easier to understand and share. It can also add a touch of professionalism to your brand.

Action Step: Create a simple visual representation of your framework.

4. OPTIMIZE: Integrate and Elevate

Now it's time to infuse your Branded UFO into every corner of your brand and business and keep on optimizing it based on customer feedback. This is how you solidify your authority and create a cohesive brand experience.

Feature your framework prominently on your website, weave it into your marketing materials, and use it as the foundation for your content strategy.

Develop workshops, online courses, or keynote speeches based on your UFO. Write a book that expands on your framework and showcases your expertise.

The more you use and reference your framework, the more it will stick in people's minds. Before long, people will start associating you with your UFO – and that's when you know you've truly become an authority.

Action Step: List three ways you'll integrate your framework into your work immediately.

Your UFO-Powered Book

Your Branded UFO can supercharge your book in several ways:

1. **Structure**: Use your UFO to organize your chapters, giving your book a clear, logical flow.
2. **Memorability**: Readers will remember your key points because they're tied to your unique framework.
3. **Application**: Create UFO-related exercises/ worksheets to help readers apply your ideas.

4. **Marketing**: Your UFO gives you a unique hook that is memorable.
5. **Spinoff Opportunities**: It makes you unique and leads to speaking gigs, courses, and consulting opportunities.

The Journey to Authority

Creating a Branded UFO is more than just coming up with a catchy name or design. It's about clearly articulating your unique value in a way that connects with your audience.

Developing our UFOs showed what made our approach special. It clarified our processes and improved our communication. Ultimately, it changed us from struggling providers to recognized authorities in our field.

Remember, your Branded UFO is your key to becoming an authority. It makes you stand out. It's what will make people remember you and seek out your expertise. As a result, you get more speaking and media opportunities.

Your journey to becoming an expert in your field starts now. A world of opportunity awaits. Simply launch your UFO and watch your influence grow!

In a noisy world, your Branded UFO is your megaphone. It boosts your voice, clarifies your message, and raises your status.

Don't just be satisfied being a part of the crowd. Be the leader, someone others admire.

Your UFO is ready for launch. The only question is: are you ready?

www.ingramcontent.com/pod-product-compliance
Lightning Source LLC
Chambersburg PA
CBHW030227100526
44585CB00012BA/285